The lie disguises. And prevents
all truth from lifting veils.
—— Chapter 6

HISTORIES AND DYNASTIES

ARLENE ZEKOWSKI

Horizon Press   ⌐⌐   New York

First Edition 1982
First Printing 1982
ISBN: 0-8180-0634-X (cloth)
ISBN: 0-8180-0632-3 (paperback)
Library of Congress Catalog Card Number: 81-85002

Library of Congress Cataloging in Publication Data

Zekowski, Arlene
  Histories and dynasties.

  (An Archives of post-modern literature series
publication; no. 106)
  I. Title. II. Series.
PS3576.E4H5   813'.54   81-85002
ISBN 0-8180-0634-X   AACR2
ISBN 0-8180-0632-3 (pbk.)

Grateful acknowledgement is made to the editors of the following
books and periodicals in which sections of *Histories And Dynasties*
first appeared: *Center, Delirium, Interstate, Voices from the Rio
Grande, Future Language, Western World Review.*

Book Design and Layout/Jean Laurence
Cover(pbk edition)/Jacket(cloth edition)/Title Pages/Herman Zaage

*Palatino, Memphis, Helvetica,
and their Italics, were used for text, with members
of Art Brush, Banco, Journal Roman and Bodoni, for display in this
book. It was printed on 60# Natural, Warren "66"
acid-free paper at Braun-Brumfield, Inc.
Ann Arbor, Michigan*

An Archives of Post-Modern Literature Series
Publication No. 106

Manufactured in the United States of America

HORIZON PRESS, 156 Fifth Avenue, New York, N.Y. 10010

BOOKS BY ARLENE ZEKOWSKI

Fiction

A FIRST BOOK OF THE NEO-NARRATIVE
CONCRETIONS
HISTORIES AND DYNASTIES

Fiction and Criticism

ABRAXAS
SEASONS OF THE MIND

Criticism

CARDINALS & SAINTS
IMAGE BREAKING IMAGES
(A New Mythology of Language)

Poetry

THURSDAY'S SEASON

Drama

THE AGE OF IRON AND OTHER INTERLUDES

FOREWORD

Language and Questioning

Welch D. Everman

LIKE PHILOSOPHY, like all of human thought, Arlene Zekowski's writings begin in wonder and amazement, and *Histories And Dynasties* is both the process and the product of her questioning. In *Grounds for Possibilities, Hemispheres, Abraxas,* and other earlier works, Zekowski began her investigations into the nature of language, human existence, and the relationship between the two, and *Histories And Dynasties* is a continuation of that lifelong effort. It is a work of possibility, and, as such, it is a questionable book in the sense that it questions both itself and its themes and, at the same time, demands to be called into question by the reader.

Histories And Dynasties is a challenge to the reader who must, in turn, challenge the work for himself. This new novel is the investigation of a mystery which cannot be resolved, but, despite the necessary inconclusiveness of the work, it is not an experiment. In *Cardinals & Saints*, a collection of essays written in collaboration with her husband Stanley Berne, Zekowski has warned against using the term "experimental" in discussing non-traditional works of art. "If we call a departure (in writing) *experimental* then we are using the wrong word. Experiment simply means, that a means to an end is being used; an end is being sought." But the work of art is not a means which might succeed or fail to reach a pre-established goal. It is an end in itself, complete, harmonious, and integral, and, though *Histories And Dynasties* is an investigation into new literary territory, it is clearly a work of art in this sense.

As an investigation, *Histories And Dynasties* poses many questions, but one question seems to be central, not only to this new work but to all that Zekowski has produced over the past thirty years.

Today the question is.
What is indeed the aspect of our lives.

This question recurs time and again in Zekowski's writings in many different forms, but neither *Histories And Dynasties* nor any of her earlier novels provide the definitive answer. They were never meant to do so. As Zekowski has written:

Answers are resolutions. Not resolves. They are finite tired old and ended. Questions are infinite tireless young and grow by

beginning. They fulfill without being fulfilled.

Art is not intended to close off thought with
answers but to inspire and perpetuate it with creative
questions that renew themselves each time they are
posed. To ask a question, even one that has been
asked many times before, is to begin again; in
Zekowski's terms, to ask is to create a "movement
[which] must go somewhere it's never been before."

The author's method of investigation is the Neo-
Narrative, the literary technique first developed by
Berne and Zekowski in the late 40's and early 50's.
Because this technique has taken different forms in
the individual works of Berne and Zekowski and because it is flexible enough to take still other forms in
the hands of other authors, it is difficult if not impossible to define the Neo-Narrative in the abstract.
The clearest explanation, of course, is to be found in
the reading of the works themselves. Still, in the
simplest terms, the Neo-Narrative is a narrative that
overrides character, plot, setting, chronology, and
the other elements of traditional fiction in favor of
language itself, a language which is free of the
artificial limits of grammar and the grammatically
correct sentence. The rules of grammar were derived
in the eighteenth century, but the eighteenth century
sentence cannot capture the twentieth century experience. As Zekowski has written in her study of
language, *Image Breaking Images:* "Grammar is not
modern just a lingering habit a form solidifying a
tradition of thinking which today is no longer true."
In the attempt to come to terms with the experiences

of modernity, Berne and Zekowski demand a break with the linearity of traditional fiction and with the linearity imposed upon language by the rules of grammar. The Neo-Narrative is that break, a technique for using words in a way that is non-linear, simultaneous, and adventurous in form and concept.

The Neo-Narrative text is not a representation of an event which, in theory, could be described in any number of ways, i.e. in different words, in a painting, in a photograph, etc. Rather, the language of the Neo-Narrative *is* the event. It is, in Zekowski's terms, "not just an abstraction which we can summarize from an experience, but is the very experience itself, constitutes its very texture."

For Zekowski, the Neo-Narrative also involves a break with the categories of literature, and her own writing makes use of prose exposition, poetic rhythms, dramatic dialogues, and a full range of techniques that reaches across traditional literary boundaries. In addition, she goes beyond the traditional materials of the literary arts to take all of man's knowledge into account. Thus, her fictions often deal directly with the facts of geology, astronomy, psychology, history, and the other natural and human sciences, as well as with more traditional areas of literary concern. The Neo-Narrative, then, is a process not for destruction but for integration; it draws upon knowledge of the past and of the present, upon tradition and the new, to create "an in-process becoming, a discovery, not a finality."

Histories And Dynasties is such a process, a wide-ranging investigation of Zekowski's central question, based on the author's astonishment at the fact that, despite his [man's] great potential and his many strengths, man has never sought the best for himself. Instead, he has developed civilizations, institutions, and nations which serve only to set him against himself. Zekowski stated the case perfectly in the foreword to her novel, *Abraxas:* "He kills what he needs. He inflicts unnecessary self-torture on himself and his kind."

Is this, then, "the aspect of our lives"? *Histories And Dynasties* investigates this question and the various possibilities for human success and failure through a comparison and contrast of civilizations and cultures from prehistory to the present. In particular, Zekowski's focus is on the United States, first because the late twentieth century has seen a global movement toward Americanization, and second because the American experience began as an effort to turn away from the self-defeating dehumanization and oppression of the past. The Americanization of the world is a fact which points to an uncertain future, because the original American dream has become open to serious question. The first Americans wanted freedom for themselves and for others; the new land was an experiment for the good of man, at least in theory. But Zekowski questions the America of the present in terms of American history. "Whether we still want. What we willed. When we arrived. Is another matter still. The one we haven't come to terms with."

Histories And Dynasties is a continual movement through time and space, from contemporary America

to ancient Greece and Rome, from Europe under
feudalism, to the North American Zuni culture, to the
prehistoric tribes of nomads that wandered over the
various continents. For the most part, this human
history is a history of war, oppression, exploitation,
and death.

So all we call ambition. The epic and
the saga of the destinies of men. Are
accidents of birth and time and place. The
situation calling for a thrust of energy and
horror. Deceiving both the victim and the
victor. Where those who win are never in
the field. Where blood and grime are. And
where life ends for some. And begins for
others.

Zekowski distinguishes between man in civilization and man in the natural world. Civilization with
its social order, its division of labor, and its technology has produced high standards of living in
every human era, but it has also produced slavery,
moral decay, and genocide, and, as a result, every
great civilization has consumed first its colonies and
its neighbors, then itself. Man stands between the
world he has made and the world as it is and would
be without him; he is part of both realms, and yet
high civilization sets him apart from "nature flesh
man god sea wind mountain valley prairie sun moon
stars continents peoples myths rituals traditions soul
spirit mortality heaven hell immortality transubstantiation." In civilization, man forgets that, as a
physical being, he cannot escape from the natural
world or exploit it indefinitely. On the other hand,

man in nature also uses the land and the animals for his own survival and benefit, but he respects the non-human world and gives to it as much as it gives to him. Zekowski's sympathies lie with this man and his time.

> . . . The time when man like animal. Was nomad. Wanderer. Like minstrel. Fanning out in bands. His groups and clans. Fixed in patterns of the weather. Like clouds that form and disappear. And merge and change. With weather. And the climate. With the stars. The moon. The setting and the rising sun. With seasons of the spirit. Of the body. Of the mind. Moving on the reflex instincts. Noble in the nature of the gesture needed. To survive meant not to hoard beyond the belly's need. So that provisions for the spirit were just as meaningful.

Still, Zekowski's respect for the man who lives in accord with nature is neither naive nor romantic, for she knows that, regardless of where and when he lives, man is always "as old as man and just as new as today." The histories and dynasties charted in this new work show that, when men band together, it is only a matter of time before they set themselves apart from the non-human world and from other bands of men. The result is prejudice, persecution, exploitation, war, and the conquest of men and of the land. The result, in other words, is man's betrayal of his human potential and of himself, and Zekowski charts the history of such human failure with a list of languages, all of them once spoken in thriving cultures, all of them now dead: Latin, Franconian, Old Saxon, Old Norse, Gaulish, Umbrian, Ionian, Sanskrit, Babylonian, Hittite, Assyrian, Coptic, etc.

The warning is clear, and yet *Histories And Dynasties* cannot provide an answer to the questions of human existence and struggle. The only "answer" is a continual questioning, something which *Histories And Dynasties* provides and inspires in the reader. The text explores the fundamental question from a variety of perspectives, and, in so doing it also explores itself and the method by which it came to be. Like so many artworks of the modernist era, like the paintings of Jackson Pollock, the music of Morton Feldman, and the choreography of Merce Cunningham, *Histories And Dynasties* exposes the process of its own creation in the product by reflecting, within the work, the making of the work itself.

The process of *Histories And Dynasties* is the act of writing, putting "a mark on something anything everything," and the author's consciousness of the act itself is built into the text. Thus, the work questions itself and its own purposes. The opening line, "Notes toward what?", sets the stage for that which is to come, and the reply, "A frame," places *Histories And Dynasties* in a context. The work is a flow of language framing the themes of the novel and framed at the same time by the pages of the volume. Again, product and process are one.

The structure of *Histories And Dynasties* is open and fluid, moving from thought to thought, carried forward not by an extrinsic logic but by the flow of the language itself. This flow often contradicts itself, but the paradoxical movement of the text is purposeful. Meaning here is not dependent upon logic, and, of course, logic could not guarantee meaning in any case. In *Histories And Dynasties,* meaning is not contained in the text like water in a bowl; rather, it is created in the act of writing and recreated in the act of reading. As Zekowski says, "the meaning of my meaning is different." The language of the text does not carry or convey or transmit a meaning; the language *is* the meaning.

Zekowski's language is distinctive and must be, because it must do more than the language of the traditional novel, i.e. it is intended not to describe or to represent, but to be. For this reason, her prose makes use of strong, often complicated rhythms, internal rhyme, and other poetic techniques. In addition, the narrative moves from first person singular to first person plural to third person to dialogue and back. The effect is quite unique. The constant flow and movement of the words leads the reader into the work, and for this reason, despite its many complexities, *Histories And Dynasties* is a highly readable text.

Zekowski moves effortlessly through the eras of history and from continent to continent, and she can do so because the form of *Histories And Dynasties* is based on the relativity of space and time and collapses the spatial and the temporal to a single, simultaneous point. In this context, all of history is available in the present, and all dynasties are contemporary. There are no beginnings or endings here, only "never endings and always beginnings."

Therefore, although *Histories And Dynasties* moves backward and forward through all of human time, it is very much a book of presence and of the present. Because, as Zekowski writes, "there's no eternal anymore," the present moment becomes the only moment of importance. Man can profit from his past, but he cannot hold only to what has been and hope to survive. "The present can not live in the past." Nor can man live only for a future time, for without a real sense of the present, the possibility of the future loses all meaning. Memories of the past and hopes for the future are significant, of course, for memory and hope, the ability to learn from what has been and to project into what will be, are what make man man. And yet living is in the now. It is the present that makes existence a reality, and man is truly man only when, with astonishment and wonder, he recognizes the gift of the living moment. "Because a present is a present."

According to *Histories And Dynasties*, man has not often made the best use of his present moments. Instead, he has persisted in choosing the past (tradition) or the future (progress) over the now. He has chosen against himself. *Histories And Dynasties* is a documentation of such false choices, and yet the orientation of this innovative book is not negative. Rather, *Histories And Dynasties* is a work of ongoing possibility. It is a free and open text, as free and open as human destiny. Man is not fated to be what he has always been, for, as Zekowski makes clear, "there is always a choice. To destiny. To fate. If you wish to choose."

W. D. E.
University of Wisconsin

PREFACE

The Ego,
the Id and the Word,
in the World of
Histories And Dynasties

Walter James Miller

WHEN YOU REALIZE that you're deep-breathing your way through a major book, you can't help making comparisons.

Because you've been there a few times before, you've lived through a few important books, your epithelium remembers other shocks like the one you're registering now.

But not exactly like. For one of the marks of a great book is that in some ways, it's a breakthrough. Earlier major works broke through problems of their times. To be really important today, a book must break through one of the barriers we've reached today.

Hence my excitement over Zekowski's new novel, her most significant book so far. It has made me live through some great but easy-to-make comparisons, with Dostoevski, Faulkner, and Heller. Better yet, it has made me feel my way through a telling contrast—with T. S. Eliot—a contrast maybe we didn't even know we were waiting for. Best of all, *Histories And Dynasties* has carried me into rare fresh air, into a newness beyond comparison and contrast.

* *

My epithelia have felt anew some of the excitements I associated with *Crime and Punishment*. What courage I took on! as Dostoevski tracked and surprised his Shadow, my Shadow, as he pioneered in lighting up dark labyrinths of inner space. Zekowski renews that courage in a time when some of us feared such lights were dimming.

Histories And Dynasties has made me think continually of *Absalom, Absalom!* How Faulkner had to invent new word patterns to float us—float himself—into that feral flux that flows in, knows no one direction, just flows and flexes: pulses. Lovers of Faulkner will cherish Zekowski.

And in reading her, I have felt something of that same joy I felt in another great breakthrough: learning, in the doing, how to experience story in *Catch-22*. Descent into Heller—as into Faulkner—meant abandoning the linear, known nowhere in Nature's adobe craftsmanship, and traveling the spiral. Zekowski too takes us through such sweeps of simultaneity.

* *

Less easily, perhaps more importantly, I have been led into a shocking contrast between *The Waste Land* and *Histories And Dynasties*. One of the greatnesses of Eliot's work lay in the lay of that Land. He invented a language—of fragments, allusions—that put his message into a medium that *is* its meaning. Fractionated people living in a brown land surrounded by dead tarry waters, we can only shore up the ruins, remember dismembered lives and works.

But the language Zekowski has invented for representing the same situation goes, it seems to me, way beyond Eliot's ambition and achievement. Zekowski's language not only pictures life in the Waste Land six decades worse. It also shows us how, in Zekowski's view, we can mix flagging memory and desire this time not for surrender but for rebirth. Eliot diagnoses. Zekowski prescribes.

Ever since the Fifties, Zekowski has maintained that it is our language itself that is suffocating us. That the traditional grammatical sentence is perfect for representing expository, analytic, logical experience. But that the sentence cannot accurately represent problems, urgings, goals of the larger psychological life.

The left brain reigns as King Arrogant so long as the logical sentence is required for expressing all aspects—even irrational aspects—of existence. The right brain—champion of intuition, lyricism, imagery—remains Serf Stultified so long as it's forced to use the King's language instead of its own.

* *

What is this other language? In Zekowski's world, a language of words patterned in bursts or pulses, usually in phrases or in clauses, sometimes even in full sentences. Zekowski aims then to make us read somewhat as we think: in Bergson's flow of discrete images, in Fromm's forgotten language.

One great advantage of Zekowski's language is that it allows us to assemble these varying word-units into our own patterns at our own pace. We free-associate far more readily—it seems to me we participate more fully—as we allow Zekowski to take us:

> Where man will reproduce. As best he can.
> The form of nature. In a form of man. Where
> nature triumphs. Even in the art of separa-
> tion in the form of mask or totem or of fetish.
> Because the creature man who made it.
> Doesn't separate the creature from the man.
> The self from the inspiration of the source.
> Are still as one. Triumphant. In the dual
> spirit rendered. Not divided and in conflict.
> As is modern man.

Notice our experience of the crucial phrase "Are still as one," which seems to fall out of nowhere. Traditional grammar tells us here *Are* is a verb that has no subject. But carried along in the feral flux, we "know" that it has. Carried along, we know how to assemble echoes: creature, man, self, inspiration, presumably all *objects* of verb and preposition, become now the compound *subject* of *Are*. The way this non-traditional "sentence" has been gathered by the reader himself takes him deeper into the thinking-feeling process than the traditional sentence could ever take us. And surely there is no hyper-romanticist surrender here of thought to feeling. Rather it is an equal partnership. Zekowski's ideas hike ahead stronger because they hike hand in hand with feelings. As *The Hudson Review* once explained her technique, it's "A device for responding directly to reality without the clumsy intervention of grammar."

* *

Zekowski involves our feelings not only by advancing meaning in suggestive clusters of words, but also by stressing meaning with shifting rhythms, assonances, half- and even full rhyme:

The augments. In the portents of their kind.

Disguising in a bafflement of gross surprise.

Like the word-bursts, the musical effects slow us down, the better to savor the experience, to contain the clusters of suggestions. Zekowski has always contended that there should be, in artistic composition, no distinction between poetry and prose.

As happens when we read *Catch-22*, we slow down too to absorb the shocks as clichés, and other familiar expressions are reversed or deflated. Zekowski writes:

> I don't see the point of calling a spade that is not a spade a spade.

> Better to have played. Than won or lost.

> Insisting better to be red than dead.

And we slow down to remember non-sentences in the happy danger of being repeated quoted repeated into tomorrow's clichés:

> To think American is to feel self-gratified. Not fulfilled. Just filled.

* *

By now you can sense the answers so I need only confirm your intuitions about these your other questions:

Zekowski's overall themes? The great book's only subjects. *Where are we? How do we get to where we wanted to be from where are we?*

Her hero-ine? You. In metaphoric guise as: the author. Zekowski's "I," like Whitman's "I," is All of Us. And sometimes, like Eliot, she breaks the "I" down into "You and I" when the Id and the Ego are arguing.

* *

If you're an accredited Zekowski aficionado, you will, I imagine, recognize this as her greatest work, a culmination, a compact synthesis of all her efforts in poetry, criticism, fiction. But if you're a newcomer to Zekowskiland, you'll want to go back now, pick up and follow her earlier trails. She first won wide acclaim, among her literary peers at least, in the mid-Fifties with two works. With Stanley Berne, she published "The End of Story in the Novel" in *New World Writing No. 11.* This now-classic essay improved the quality of the air we breathe. It shook up the literary world and got us thinking anew about the obsoleteness of our fictional forms and textures. It helped draw attention to that other Berne-Zekowski triumph of that period, *A First Book of the Neo-Narrative,* which demonstrated in practice what the essay set down in theory. *Neo-Narrative* included appreciations by William Carlos Williams and Donald Sutherland. Since the Fifties, other leading critics—from Sir Herbert Read to Richard Kostelanetz—have kept us aware that many advances made by the last two generations of avant-garde writers have been predicted *and* paced by Zekowski and Berne. Zekowski's *Abraxas* appeared in 1964 and her *Seasons of the Mind* in 1969. Her *Image Breaking Images,* advocating a return in literature to a "grammarless language," stirred up a storm in 1978, a storm that tore through many editorial pages and even through the U.S. Senate and *The Congressional Record*. These are crucial works in a long bibliography of Zekowski publications. Together with her masterpiece, *Histories And Dynasties*, Zekowski's output gives us many a happy chance to breathe once more as we have breathed through Dostoevski, through Faulkner, through Heller—deep, fresh, revitalized.

W. J. M.
New York University

HISTORIES AND DYNASTIES

So thus. The patterns of behaviour. And belief. As linked we are to one another. And to time. And change. And histories and dynasties.

— Chapter 20

ONE

NOTES TOWARD WHAT? A frame.

The artist finds the thing he seeks. Even tho it isn't there. He is human. He makes. Along the lines the forms the colors. Of the addled symbol in his brain? Perception maybe.

How can we as fishers lie. Beneath the net. Avoiding all captivity. As seen by man. The inward feel of life. Of warmth. Of riverine and oceanic form. The depth of dark and liquid in the mass. We are. As only fishers know.

It's all a jakes this world. We're privy to it

all. And all our private parts as well. Appalled. We revel in the stench we cannot stand. A contradiction to ourselves. The mystery of life as smell. But mystery nevertheless still.

In the other eons of my lives as I or someone else. I wonder now as maybe yes or no. I did before. I'll never know. Did it all regurgitate revulsions about the time the ripe fruit had to fall? As the bough bent. So the tree. As the seed. As the flower. So the fruit.

I find the consciousness.
Of this my present moment. Quakes. In wonderment. Amazed and terrified. Of what I've hoarded in the 2 year putting aside of pen to paper.

So the bird flies.
Not well but awkwardly.
But at least it flies.
So what?

This is the taunt your life takes when you've reached the middle of the struggle.
You wonder what it is that is so special about being a writer, a "serious" writer at that.

You've done your best.

But best is not enough in terms of the forever of this life in this your present eon.

I turn the page.

The page is/was blank. So time flies and is used.

The pen put to the page. The words falter. In a kind of shiver of parturition. As if your hoard you can't decide is something found and made. By you. Or that other from which you derive. The fright. The hesitation. Muffled cry. And pain. The pain is mystery. Because it mystifies you. And prevents the sentient being in you. From knowing. Ever understanding. What the pen describes.

To describe. Is to make a picture. But suppose there are blinders on the perception markers and targets of your brain.

This moment which is never frozen. Ages into the future. So that this present never is. But onwards. It rejects itself. Spews its lie. In the very truth sincerity of its feel. It feels its now. But Now is somewhere else. In Future let's not talk of past or present. They're always just divisions. The rationales of this our sadist brain. To put a mark on something anything everything. And momentarily to call a halt. To freeze the picture so to speak. While life and death proceed and recede. So that measuring is out. It's meaningless.

I'll end that thought or suspend it. For another. There's nothing else. No other but a new alternative. If we move we stay awake. Even tho we may be dreaming. We'll never know in this our "swinging" present.

I am a writer.
Well what of it.
Who cares?

There's a revolution in print on the West Coast of this pestiferous country. San Francisco, Laguna, Venice, Los Angeles, San Diego, La Jolla. Even San Clemente. All up and down the Pacific. In the California sun and smog. The grovelling ants are crowding each other with their burdens. On which they prop their pens and feed. Cry revolution counter-culture 3rd World (Hopi in origin?) Lesbian Fag Lama cult Chicano Brown Beret, Afro-pseudo-americano Panther, Sly Pornographer Indian Powerers Mother Earthers Rolling Stones. Against the downtrodden WASPS transformed transmogrified into Jewish Intellectuals a mutation *marriage de convenance.*

Well I don't see the point of calling a spade that is not a spade a spade. You do it. Not me.

Which means using curse words political words, racist words porno words, poetry words, prose words, and all the other words words words of label category definitions and calling it Poetry. Or Literature. When all it is is. Words Words Words. As Hamlet says.

Which brings me to another matter. That's plagued me all this life. As author-creature with pen in hand. Aching. To cry. Aching. To laugh. And sometimes. Just Aching. A kind of nameless undefined hell.

I don't think that Letters in future will be concocted from old rhythms and skins and blood and guts and dreams and pangs and joy laughter tears primordial hates loves fears wants poverties riches of the reaching back heresies and heritages of our gaunt grisly saged God-in-Man and Man-in-God forefathers of book-writings that made culture and civilization and all those other connective anathemas of our slavish peevish torture-loving senile maso-sadist word-worshippers.

There will be new priests. As Whitman said. Here I seem to be contradicting myself. But no. I can't see these priests as poets. Which is what Whitman meant. But I do not.

What then do I mean?
Well it depends on your values.
It depends on whether you can try the impossible. Well have not Poets tried the impossible. I myself have said they have. And must continue to. But now I contradict as Whitman said and I do now. But the meaning of my meaning is different. Hold on. Not so fast. So impatient. Slow down. And think.
Priests as poets cannot be. Poets are not priests and priests not poets.
Even tho each thinks he is.
The priest predicts. The poet fore-shadows like any artist with his tools. But neither is a sage today. We can no longer believe their feel. We can no longer feel their belief. We disbelieve. But we do feel even tho we disbelieve the old feels and the old beliefs.

Now comes the problem.
Or how to solve the impossible.
How does a poet-priest or priest-poet,
regain our confidence?
He doesn't. Not in the old way at least.

What I am writing now is conscious. Deliberate. But in a new way. At least for the present. The artist-poet-priest must turn. Not like the worm he was. The clown freak of the crowd. Aping the crowd. And the crowd's values. He must rise on his bruised haunches. And totter and limp into the wilderness. Not like Moses or like Christ waiting for God's word in them. Ah no.

But he must find words.
Well yes.
Well?
Well not words as such.
Experiences?
In a way.
How you equivocate!
Hesitation shows my necessary faltering
to describe the new.
What new?
Dare I say what I feel?
No one else will.

That's true.

Well state it then.

It's easier to illustrate but that's the old way. Don't state. Illustrate. Perhaps no statement. No illustration. Just an erasure towards suggestion.

A contradiction in logic!

Yes, I know. And yet the truth must be suggested in order to be recognized.

What truth?

A whole new logos shall we call it, of Art.

TWO

THE MYSTERY IS WHAT we shall call it.

Mystery?

Yes to find the seed the germ sensation of the creature in creation of the life as new and strange and never to be before even as the human in us reels as centuries of the eons past present future. Do you ponder?

Yes but what?

What about?

What is *it*?

To try again again again to seize upon and on and on the many blanks I draw and draw again as dreams the nightmares lurch destroying and creating all I've ever known or travelled by, the psyche of the soul the essence of the art-song thing of ugliness of beauty revelation not for me as such but thru me as it jabs and shimmers as I shiver as I cry, the pain relief, the flow in substance like a river the clog the suffocation failure and return until the jettison that bursts the wall of dike as mystery returns to mystery in blinding flashes in the dark and fear illumined struggle and revulsion and relief and dully in a conscious or self-conscious self the self returns oblivious to the self as seed to be blows chokes dust the void return to void as nowhere gropes and gropes and knows not what it seeks afraid of words afraid afraid afraid.

The poet has been never "fraid" of words.

But this one is I am I am I am.

In this you reach your being do you not?

Sometimes sometimes.

Not always?

No not always. The thread again. You see. No longer what it was. I shudder now to say to try to say.

If I say *what*? it will not help.

No because specifics are what poets feed upon. The staff and stuff of life. The bread.

The bread.

Yes. But new bread. I want to make new bread. No longer beer or maize or mead. No Beowulf epic of the old remembered myth race memoried in a vague ancestoried return. To darkness time. Of every peopled person's mythy mind. Which poets seize upon. And breathe like gods upon it. With their words. No words of recognition any more. For future of the time that's been. Your brow it furrows in confusion?

Yes I do not understand. If not to recognize then how can you or I or anyone relate man essence to ourselves or others?

It's what I'm trying to explain.
There's no eternal anymore.

You sound like an oracle would. A mystery. Unclear.

It is unclear. And just as frightening. Like an oracle you said. Because the language of our speech relation must have movement. And movement as we know it goes somewhere. But I am trying to reach you and even myself, above all myself but just as much you, with movement that contradicts itself.

Why?
Well it, the language, the movement must go somewhere it's never been before.
Like going to the moon perhaps.
Perhaps. But that voyage connects with man as he is because it's monitored. It's an old path

even though the direction seems strange surreal unreal. And the passengers in the modules are nothing more than bus boys are they not. No poets or newtons or einsteins no painters no composers. Just anthropoid vulgus man robot-like pavlovian and uncomplex carrying out logarithm-like complexities programmed and soulless. Why not a poet or a Varese tune his rhythms into quasars or whatever those mysteries of star eons are called.

Someday.

Well I mean now. To use my power or hunger to know what I don't know to try the impossible as yet gesture of defiance at a god-reach of definition of 2000 years of man and god perfectly mythologized to suit man of his divinity and the poet of his, the seer he's supposed to be, the priest of words of emotion of experience, the petroglypher and mnemonic Homer of the first epic and all the others after. Virgil Beowulf Dante Milton and all the obscure forgotten moth-eaten scholar-kissed exhumations of dead and Byzantine dross-pustuled emanations of pancreas-livered bile blown indigestible and undigested narcissistic mumbo-jumbo rituals of tradition-gutted-man. His brains are blown you know. He's finished as he is the sot.

Who? The poet?

Yes. Man. And man poet. And Letters as they are. Past. Present. Unless you're a worshipper of things as they are or have been.

Where do you begin to change it all? It seems impossible insane. The mistakes as you'd call them.

All existence is about mistakes. Why should Art as we know it be our only mistakes?

Why indeed? I don't follow.

I want to try others. What you, I, history might prove as mistakes just as I state as I'm reiterating to you now without shame shock or qualms that creativity in man thru his story his accounting of himself on the records of this planet has led to zero.

Zero? Nothing? We'd all contradict you.

And prove me wrong you think?

Yes.

In the present context of things as they are as Mathew Arnold said having destroyed himself as a somewhat poet having tried having failed, dreadfully, abominably, having hidden it, the fact, the knowledge the realization from himself and having yes somehow unwittingly discovered it, it killed him.

Well, in Mathew Arnold's case, perhaps, but not in every case in the past.

No, as the vigor remains and gives life to life as Letters did but no longer does. You see you recognize the distortion the lie in Mathew Arnold's case.

The lie to himself?

The lie to himself and the lie to humanity. To believe in the past when the present had no future. The present can not live in the past.

True to a degree. But why didn't "the present [have] no future," that is, in Mathew Arnold's time?

Because it was repeating itself.

But doesn't all life have a kind of cyclic repetition and recognition as perhaps the Jungians might say or imply?

Yes. But in nature when a species has completed, has served its purpose the cycle does not, is not continued by nature. It's either abandoned or is traced to something else, like the evolution and dissolution of primitive *Protista* lacking organized nuclei and tissue systems which decreased carbon dioxide and increased oxygen and ozone of 3 billion years ago.

But this this *Protista* as you call it is no concern of mine.

Protista is a botanical definition. And concerns us all. The primitive *Protista* prepared for life as we know it as algae protozoa and fungi know it. As the artist knows it. There are no more *Protista*. There may be soon no more man no more art unless they evolve into something else. Doomsday is no longer myth but a possibility.

> Why?
> Because man because art because culture civilization are played out. Tired of repeating themselves tired of believing the anthropomorphic drivel drone of pre- and post-lapsarian adamic ego-jacketed schizoid man. He suffers from acedia and needs an analeptic. He's blown his mind.

THREE

CONTINUATION OF THE TIME'S becoming sometimes answers.

We change roles or stances. I see you
poetize.

I sometimes try to. To try to understand
what those who face and speak of soul can render.

They knead like bakers. Making things.
It's their reason of being.

But so do scientists as well.

As well yes. Not the same.

What difference is there?

In the making of the poet as against the
other the scientist?

Yes.

For one thing. Soul. Imagination creative
drive may be the same. But one can have imagination
without soul. The scientist yes. The poet no. He must be

means and ends and spirit of the life we lead evoking to us its existence.

But don't we know we all exist?

A metaphysical question. Descartes' attempt was to define it. Nothing more.

Why nothing more? It satisfied the mind for centuries. Western mind.

Perhaps. But mind as mind? Nothing but fulfillment of the ego. It's not enough for poets and for man-humanity as such. To satisfy to compliment the mind because we know its somewhere there. Related to the brain.

I see. Or rather do not understand. But grasp it somehow.

How?

Well perhaps by feeling you are right. There's something to what you say about the non-fulfilling mind. Like leaving you with ownership. Not possession.

Exactly so. And somewhat of a paradox. Possession's of sensation. Sensuous. The feeling of a grasp. Ownership's the statement of a fact. Not proof.

Like Thoreau defined between the personal. That you owned in the soul's possession. Its intrinsic worth. Not extrinsic value. As put upon the world.

Exactly. The poet. If he functions. Occupies the soul. Transmits it. To others who receive. Because the poet defines.

What?

Why. Everybody's world of man. The greatest poets do. Have done. Up to this crucial hour of no return.

No return to what?

To past forms and shapes and definitions of the human. In their colorings of red white black yellow. The future will be different. As the present is becoming in a change.

How can something be becoming. It either is or isn't. Isn't it?

Rhetorical but not true. It's an evolution if you can hover like a hummingbird over its object. It's a point of view. Really a perception. I've written of before. In. *Seasons Of The Mind.* The visual being only a means to perception. One of many means. Many see. But don't perceive. The simple analogy of Oedipus and Tiresias. Is limited. But classical. A beginning only, for humanity. We have a long way to go. To begin to grasp with all our potential. It's why the poet is important. Has always been. And will be. Producing a field. In the electrical sense. But going beyond it. A vast sensorium. Where we vibrate to responses. Like the hummingbird. So to speak. In a state of suspension. Because movement is difficult to define. From Zeno the Eleatic to Bergson. In the mathematical logical-oriented-trained brain way of man. As Bergson says ". . . movement is made up of immobilities." The absurdity of logic to define parallel contradictory and simultaneous. Because they can't grasp the *field*. The *texture*. The multi-dimensional anti-rational nature of flowing perceptions. What the poet describes if you will. And the scholar tries to define in his loose over indulged critiqueism. What he calls *ambiguity*. Ambiguity is milk-sopism. Hiding behind analysis that doesn't render. That delivers you back to the conundrum of life. Is Milton's Satan easier to relate to than Adam? Or are we all Adam and Satan? Or are the Christians right in insisting we must be Adam even if we're not, for the sake of society, of civilization? Or is everybody's clue-in to *Paradise Lost* or to Genesis right and wrong or all right or all wrong? Whatever, the poet has rendered the field. And that's more important than questions or answers. Because it has a life of its own. A soul. The poet does not resolve paradoxes. He presents them. The scientist the scholar are full of imagination but no soul. They insist on solutions. They insist on function. Not germination and flowering. They have always been antiseptic. They are always cleaning up the manure. The cultures. Isolating the cultures. The poet is not immune to infection. He takes on the disease of life. Lets it grow inside him. With all its fever dirt infection. Lets life take its course. Lets the nature of it be. Like the nature it is. From whence it comes. To that it's going to.

Organic to itself and others. To beginnings and middles and endings. And to never endings and always beginnings. To its own flow and genius. So that we recognize the poet's field. Authentic to its substance. Of its substance. Never perhaps the same. But always true to the substance and essence of the field. Which fluxes with the current of its own life. As we with ours. Which so often corresponds to or is the poet's field. And so we are fulfilled by him alone. Who is the spokesman in his art. For this our life.

FOUR

I'VE TRIED TO DIALOGUE myself.
Like splitting an atom.
Dangerous.

Conscious/Unconscious. The me. The thou. The it. That comes between us. The juggernaut. As energy expunged. Denies us entry into self. And others.

I shall be alone now.
Trying to repair the split self. In a unity we would believe.

The split returns reintegrating integers.

Energy discharged. And used. As pain heals wounds. The cry of grim. As cast for limb. The broken tendon-muscle. In the modulation of the shimmer shiver blood. As coursing charged. Like vapours and mists. The marl in shards of broken slivers. Where bone meets bone. To graft the self together.

Consciousness is often pain. Awareness being. Like a weight of leaded matter. Migraining over everything.

All but sting.

Divided as we are. The birth and pang. Reality resumes. The dreams that fracture. And that reel us. Into cauterizing pain.

What sift.

As like a light. Fragmented on its own beams. Flying.

Fall. As need. The moth of you or I. As burnt crisp. In all renewal. Like a phoenix gesture. Hoping to be reborn. The flail. The tired hasps upon the spring. Drawn. Waiting to sing. Assail the door closed vault of memories and new beginnings.

Gender into dreams. The substance rendered shimmer. As all flesh creeps. As river ringing.

The regurgant sound of pebbles on the air waves. Into solid. Into liquid falling. The rhythm beating rhythm. The groping modulations of the lines and circles. Onto forms.

Shapes. The threefold messenger. As I. My parts and persons. Shake your hand in mine. Which is part yours. Part mine.

We are as silent airwaves of the future. Soul on soul. Bounding off its essence like a star in outer space. Our quasar modulations interpenetrate. Disturb. But leave no messages behind. The substance of our void communication. Alone and gone.

Why vary.
With the substance of our seekings.
As we try identities that seem new to us.
Destruction is the essence of a way not natural.

I cannot play roles.
I cannot play. I must be natural.
Whatever it is to enjoy the feel of what it is to be. Even the pain. Even the cloying ego. Even the

shame of being human. With regrets of weakness and of strident rage and all disharmonies.

As we void attempts to love each other. Acting the opposite of what we feel. Then we kiss and are ashamed. As the children of spirit we are.

Man is not aristocratic in his rages. In his sudden storms. Of meaningless and unstructured energy gone wild.

Berserk in nature is another thing.
Moreoften not berserk.
Like the quiver of the lightning. A gesture on the weathering sky. A pen stroke of the artist on the page. But not the same. Even in comparison. The full explosion is a surfeit of long containment. As we gesture it to stop. But on it goes. The rain. The thunder. Exhausting itself. Its rage. A full renewal. A plenitude that foisons air and earth. Until it satisfies. Fulfills. And is fulfilled.

A human rage is not the same you see. I needn't flash the details which we recognize.

You cannot sing. You cannot fly. All the time. There are moments that are fruitless. As well as fruitful. This is a gray day. After a long gray night of rain. In a vast southwestern sky of gray cloud cumulus. After a long dry summer of drought.

It is difficult to open and unfold in the onslaught of moisture. One is breathless to catch the oxygen. Four thousand feet above the level of the sea. On an inland desert steppe.

I find the danger is in reading literature. Before I pick up my pen.

I don't mean science or philosophy or myth or history or geology or biography. I mean literature. It robs my soul. Reading another soul exposed. I can't expose my own. It's as if space and air and my essence were denied me. Like the primitive who fears the camera. How can he be he. When another tries to reproduce him. As the poet robs me of my own. When he occupies the space that I would move in for the moment. And find myself pushed aside. Substituted for a page of print. Like the photo does the primitive. Trying to capture his soul. And making him feel confined. I understand. I've been there before myself. We are all brothers in our fears and superstitions and our instincts. They never lie. I mean. The feelings.

FIVE

THESE TIMES ARE FOR the realities of dreams.

To call upon as evocations of desire.

Though not quite sure of fixed upon as seen.

Envisioned in the darker reaches of our souls.

Denied of access to the will. The hidden body politic. To mind fulfilling action.

Wherefore. Then again why not. Demand that privacies be given all their play. To halt the crudities of non-think. From explosion and impulsion. Onto everywheres of every semi-reach invasion of our many selves. So star-crossed in the effort to disgorge. Whatever of digestion we have swallowed and consumed.

So what we are. Returns to offal. In a plague of infestations. Shreds and morsels of remorse. The undigested shreds of time. As wastrel magottings of thought-rejections. In our island voyagings. Exploratory of ourselves and others. As we delve down. Swimming thru our brain cells. And siphon off the blood coagulations of our sensitivities. More often clogged and stagnant. In repressive motions. Of our flailing-failing movement. To conform our actions. To conformity on stage.

Conformity however. Notwithstanding. Seems more than what it is. And so extracts the viper-vampire of itself a seeming mode of hunger and of fear. With all shades drawn. Behind. Before. And after. And within. To unplug you and me. From every wired gesture of vibration. That wants to sing. Electrical. Or lyrical. Or both. To be. In the plasma of its own awakening. Conformity never knows is always there.

Quiescent then is life. Waiting for erection and seminal. Green as the fused flower. In the light of factories of food in nature's time. Struggling for infusion. And diffusion. As languid-longing. As a maple-leaf. For food. And air. And water. As the light restoring. Into action and renewal of itself. The life and full gestation. Engendered into form.

Conformity is then a tension. Fully to be felt. Resolved and broken in turn. By turn of will and wanting. As fulfillment in a harmony of one's own making. Incapable of being but itself.

So here I try the resolution of my soul. In full and fraught extension of this my middle-guard of years. In silence and in growth of self. As person and as author. Unknown to both many and to few. With just an occasional reverberation in the way of contact.

Praise or blame as opposites of feeling. Is what is sometimes coveted. If only to feel felt. The words. The words. The words.

What puzzles and what shocks and pains. Is the time-in-life extension of ourselves. Where receivership acceptance. Seems at least another planet range time away. So that all life and substance of the poet that you are. Is an anthem of ironics in reverberation. Where your audience-assembly of your soul and thought and feeling-being. As the distillation of so many others. Ready to acquiesce-response in any way they would. And can. Is always present and tensile. Quivering for contact. Yet starved. In the miasma of solitude. In the wall-blind protection. The oasis of isolation we form around the self. The never-knowing angst and sure conviction. Quivering to be refuted. That we are quite alone. Unique in our own tragedy of blind unknowing. In a world unknown. Known only by all its unknown quantitites. As enigmatic to us as we to it.

While the poet wishes it could be otherwise. He justifies his own conviction. That it someday will. And writes his contact of the life he knows and lives. And hopes existence in the work expressed. Will meet existence in other lives. That need his own. For proof they have not lived in vain. Nor life nor being of a man or woman. The vanity Koheleth felt it was.

This time is not a time for poets. Tho more than ever. Than before. Like ants in ant hills. Grovelling for grub. Antennas of life and feel. They scream and blind you with their singed snarls of pain. And think because they've suffered. And declared their suffering. They've diplomaed into POETS.

Suffering does not make poetry. Life is suffering. And suffering is knowing that you're alive. But a poet must be more than the "suffering servant." The Job. Or Christ. Or Buddha. He must know he is a poet. Not a sufferer. He must be a paradox unto himself and others. He must create. Even where creation is denied. Even when creation is forbidden. He must make the impossible live. And make LIFE. Out of impossibility. He must show existence. Where existence is denied. He must be inevitable. He or She. And thus find acceptance.

When Dante placed Virgil in Limbo. He didn't know it was a place for all poets. Including himself.

Paradise is not our lot. As a permanent condition. Only an aspiration. The life of the poet. No different than the life of any and all of us. Finds its existence in limbo. And finds existence itself a limbo.

It is difficult to accept limbo. Since we would deny ourselves uncertainty. As we grovel in it all our lives. With our dying breath. We shall deny it exists. As we struggle towards a conviction. That we can assail and conquer. Mystery. And the Unknown.

With Gertrude Stein. It is better to ask. What is the question. Because if anything. The poet knight-errants. In a maze of quests. Answers are resolutions. Not resolves. They are finite tired old and ended. Questions are infinite tireless young and grow by beginning. They fulfill without being fulfilled. They are the proper mode of life-longing for poets. Questions create and reveal. Answers deny and conceal. Questions and Answers are essentially antipodes. They will never meet.

SIX

THE RITUAL OF PEN to page.

Intent and savage in a pent up fire. Not to drown alive in burnings unconsumed. The raw flesh fury. Blind alive. As dead in life and on. We struggle to make sensibility. Of sense. As meaningful. As cells within us breathe. And feed the flow. Together with all nurture. Of the brain. And soul.

The sweat. As wanton in its play of spirit feeding. Over and again. To ply. As surge upon the surge. The oiled nut screw. Of cap upon the piston circulation. Firing the reason out. And pressing like a book press on its clasp. The surge of flow. To muster. Like a river breaking all the winter cap of frozen surface.

Now to rise. Unworthy to the onslaught of all that's worthy. As true to find awhile. Remembrance. And the living of the present moment. True to cause and entry folding.

The difficulty is always gestured on the consciousness. That which we would as fully as assert. Without the knowing of the blinding revelation. Contradictory to self-assertiveness. Not negative. Not positive. A thing of self. Asserting being.

As for try. The will denies. The fathoms. As so dark and bleak we are. Of spirit wanting. Wanting to be spirit taken. And spirited away to nowhere. Are we there. Wherever place and stance is. For the rhythm of the all that surges and regurgitant as spume. White water chopping. Anger of clenched fist fears. Of being. As the being. In the spirit being. Devours every vestige of the onslaught of denial.

Denial is self. Denying self. So how to live this life of lie about us. In Society. And government in life. And Government. The lie disguises. And prevents all truth from lifting veils. The mask preferred. Is always dead and motionless. And always silent. In the recognition we would all deny.

The topical is full of tension. Speeches proclaim. Confusion reigns. We must obey. The dollar is in crisis. So is spirit. But matter is what we feed on. Not the spirit. We must keep things in motion. For possession is the water gauge of our human nurture. Whether we will or no. Possession reigns and rains. The flesh of human recognition. And of contact. The dross communication of our lives. Misunderstandings in the brotherhood of man. In family machinations of the clan. Extend to nationhood as pride in self. Identity is lost to view. We hide ourselves. And laugh away our fears. In clown subservience. To the vulgus. Who is animal and feeds his non-think. In distractions spiriting whatever spirit quiver recognition of the vanity of this our lives. Into blind obeisance to the god Frivolity.

The modus vivendi of vulgus americanus. Is always the clean slate. The tabula rasa. He wants no clutter to his life. Except clutter. Non essentials are the key to unlock his trunk of tricks up the sleeve. The slap on the back comraderie of common denomination. Is his notion of nationhood. Of being and feeling American. Of sameness in diversity he doesn't see. Or wish to see. Let the god all things equal be. Equal all things. Equal or not. It all fits into the common mold. Because we make it fit. Bread without germs of wheat. Wine without body and bouquet. Fruits and vegetables mass harvested in bumper crops that are leached of vitamins. All sacrificed to the need for plenty. For equality of feed for all.

We drown our taste in beer of arrested fermentation. We love additives to glut and clog our drains. Our feces lacks organic substance as it slides in drains. And flushes into septic tanks. To be septic is our symbol of redemption. From the unclean irregularity of individual idiosyncracy. It is indeed idiotic to be different. Even though we countenance long hair and calico gypsy indian nuances of outlandish color and textures. And deliberately patched slob style harlequin aplomb. And tattered style pathfinder leather jerkins. And Afro hirsuteness on wasp calvin disoriented caucasians. What the h___. We're all the same. Underneath the granny glasses. The marijuana hashish heroin syndrome. The strobe lights. The rock folk jazz. The sentimental MAKE LOVE NOT WAR. The Hippies. The Freaks. No different from their ancestoried before brothers. The beatniks. The bobby soxers. The zoot suiters. All wanting to be different. Yet the same. The collective evangelism of America. Is always with us. The god of conformity rains conformity. As conformity reigns in nonconformity. A mask is a mask. And we are the people. The nation as players. We always play. We run. We never walk. We jump. We don't stand still. Pretension and disguise. We pretend we are great. We disguise our need for solitude. Which is never fed. Stillness is wasteful. Action is all. Strike while the iron is hot. Burn your hand. Then hide your tears of pain behind the mask. American.

      The child of action and impulse. To think American is to feel self-gratified. Not fulfilled. Just filled. Stuffed with the surplus harvests of demineralized foods. Gorged with the artifice of subliminal pavlovian obeisance. To the god of our GNP. How apt our god label. The Gross National Product. What a deity of dead descent we have come to worship. We Americans who would have no ghosts. No traditions of ancient repressions of shreds of history. Of love of place. We love no place. We move to the rhythm of security. Of soothing insurance and pensions and fringe benefits. We love frills. The cream on the cake. Wine with the sugar added. Additives in cream cheese and chili dips. And quick soups canned with botulism. And sausages with grain additives. And meat cured and softened by chemicals. We love novelty and experiment. We hate Nature. The rhythm of family and nation genesis. The maturation of age and time and place and structure. Of kings and castles and suavity and sophistry and nobility. All this we hate. We would be always new never old always young. We worship violence. And find it romantic. Our knight is never King Arthur. Only the fisticuff roistering cowhand on his end of week tavern binge. The bushwacker. Not the civilizer. We hate civilization. We hate goodness. Though we think we believe in goodness and equality. We just want to be equal and the same. We want still to be low. Subservient. Like we were in the old country. From which we rebelled. But the reason for rebellion has escaped us. Only rebellion. We escape from our escape in rebellion. In violence. Our momentum has never ceased. But our reason for the momentum has long been lost. We just gyrate. Fluctuating on the tightrope of our nerves. Our nervous energy purposeless without audience but ourselves. All actors in a jig of fools. Sacrificing ourselves to the circus of the farce of our culture our disease-ridden civilization.

SEVEN

THE CONDIMENTS OF THESE our pleasures past.

Belaying us above the chasms of our true temptations. Dizzying the thrust for fall. The natural inclination of the mind that swerves between its own. As power granted to remove or change. And other forces darkening. As all obscurity wins over after all.

What but rim. The tide. The limitation sweep of power surge. As antechamber. To the passions. And the rages inward. As the clenched fist. Whitening to knuckle bone. Will not give over. And release its grasp upon itself.

The sundry of our casts for hue.

For sum and substance of the meaning of ourselves. Our coloration pigment on the full vibration of our spot of time. In space projection in its own trajectory. Of this our lives. The moment now or never. To be borne into or onto. In the essence of the self engaged.

To try.
The slowly of fulfillment urged.
By what. By other than impediments the skill. Impending in expression of the dream as urged.

What dreams can do. A history of religions can surely tell. The revelations of the onslaught will. And passions urged. Impinged upon. By other than the self so smitten.

As was the woman called "Ambrosia" from Athens. In one eye blindness mocking at the cures in Epidaurus. The disbelief a fright and hope in doubt. Of whether Apollo and Asclepius. Could and in deed of fact. Did cure. Or was it fancy of a wish fulfillment. That caused her dreams to sweep away the mockery of day. That moved her lips to utter: "It is unbelievable and impossible that the lame and the blind can be made whole by merely dreaming!" But then when sleep transformed her moment of suspension into dream. She dreamed of all her wishes to be made whole. Where god in dream returned the fervency of her desire. Demanding she bequeath him with a silver pig. In remembrance of her blind stupidity. And so he cut and drugged her eye. And came the day. She went forth cured.

How to urge upon ourselves.
Whatever substance of the self so tried.
In every form we justify for sure.
When surety is just bravado of the will.
That hides behind its own façade.

The masks we wear. As heirs to this our momentary thrust. Of culture in its full asseveration. Are trials of games gone wild. To prove we would know all and do. Of every aspect of the games we play.

So delicate is art and life. The jig-saw balance of negation and assertion. In ignorance and darkness as we probe for forms of knowing and for living.

The Koyemshi, the Mudheads of the Zuni. Are kin to everything that was and is burlesque. The satyr ribaldry of the early Greeks. The goat play like the mudheads of the Zuni. All in seriousness. The comedy burlesquing all our cant.

For truth must be a laugh. The grand guffaw. The kingdom of this planet Earth. Reverberates. As when it shakes and shivers. And sends tremors. Via monsoons tidal waves and quakes. And all that man can do is make the record speak. And not convey security or appeasement. He expiates his sins by recordings on the Richter scale. The seismic forces emerge as numbers graphed. And all we have is intensity on a grand scale recorded.

And so we ply our way between among disasters. Never knowing quite just what we want. But wanting what there is to want. Whatever in material is available. Stuffing our frights and fears and insecurities with things, with objects that are mouthed and bellied in our wild and grim consumption. We would devour not digest. Digestion's slow and there's no time. We catch our breath and gasp our lives away. Running away from life and death alike. Moving in the gestures of a silly dance. Gesticulating without deliberation. In a frenzy of ourselves we've formed.

Whereas the Zunis have their Koyemshi, their mudheads. To communicate their harsh laughter of their world and others worlds. And so their bellowings and screams and paroxysms. Laughter Tears Anger Despair and so on. Strike home. Response residing in a full complacency of universal understanding and acceptance. Amongst the other Zunis. And in kind.

Where we as anglos cannot understand. Where we succeed. And where we don't. We play at clowning all the time. But don't succeed. We cannot seem to exorcize the devil of play and naughtiness in us all. And thus be liberated like the Zunis or the early Greeks of the creation of tragedy. But we americanos gesture the laugh and muster the tears. But cannot give ourselves to either. We do not dominate the action. Having lost the act of choice. Which insecurity enforces. In surrender to our G N P. As Mephistopheles to Satan. So we as Faustian to Mephistopheles. We've crossed the line that separates theater from reality. And as a people we're all theater. Not reality. And cannot even enjoy the gory entertainment. We've provided for ourselves.

EIGHT

THE CREATURE COMFORTS of our time.

Are those that would expose us to ourselves. To sell and barter for the rights and privileges. The grand design. Which conquests of the mind and spirit know not of. To launch upon our decade's taunts. And bribes. And schemes insulting us. In degradations little dreamed of. In the pride and confidence. Of a culture seeding. Which ultimately. Of itself. Has gone to seed.

Where are we then.

We Kings. We Commoners. Who strut like peacocks. Our neon scapes that scream. That shout the blasts of color. As we singe ourselves with turning into nowhere circles. As we paw the dust of centuries. Which minutes. Even seconds. Have surpassed. In horror. The badge of blood. Of honor and bravado. And of *courtoisie*. Noblesse oblige. King Arthur. And the Black Prince. All in one. Have gone. Their cerements and ceremony. The brass plaques. Arresting us to gaze upon their shapes and forms. Wrested from the death's head. Of bone and ash and dust and dissolution. Into symbols of the monuments. Which time will almost leave alone.

But we. Inheritors of centuries. That plunged. Immersed in guilt and glory. And the gilt preserved. The stains of blood Pilate-like. Emerged. Submerged. And risen. The resurrected forms. And prayers of shame. And hidden prides and shreds of angers blown. Like winnowed wheat. Where all the chaff is trampled on. And driven off. And nothing but the dry dust. And the wind remains. Where bread was made. And broken. Like a covenant broken. And a promise violated.

Where we. As conquerors of present conflicts. Much and many of our own devising. How we sow. So the saying goes. So then shall reap. The same in kind. And quality of no return.

Our harvests are like dry sand. Blowing aimlessly where earth will not receive. Because there is no reservoir of matter or of seed. To pull down and to root. And send upward. A green life. A nourishment for us all.

We are as symbols of a certain longing unfulfilled. Which would cry treason. To ourselves and kind. And ask our fathers and our grandfathers. And so on. Down the line of change. Transference from the European to American. Where did they go wrong.

Wherever. In whatever form. Descendants have a way of breeding inward. Along the line of genesis. The genes they have been granted to encourage.

So here we are. The children of a dream gone sour. Ripening in a grim mutation of the children of the hope and promise. Of the full deflation. Quite unfulfilled. The energy snuffed from under our gay rambunctious fun loving balloon. Which never got off the ground.

At least not the way we had hoped.

The Eldorado of our sidewalks paved with gold. For every peasant of a European substance. To transform himself. Like Cinderella from the pumpkin. In a celebration. Of joy and comfort and of riches without end. That would never end.

Until this moment. In our dull sad thud of now we pay the piper. As our Everyman receives the burden of his life's commitments. The centuries we've struggled in the aimless muck and mire. Praying to the god. And shouting to the world. Our progress. Proclaiming the success of recusancy. Grinning from ear to ear. In our rebel shout and taunt. How cleverness is clever. How "know-how" knows how. To do what? To be what? A doer and a maker of a certain kind. A tinker shouting his wares. Screeching into the eyes and ears of all. Into the mouths and bellies. Pouring his hardware. And wondering why it never lasts longer than the bombs we also make and sell. And broadcast. In the power of the flipped switch. Which arranges death and slaughter. By remote control.

We've improved the rhetoric of war. No longer emblazoned in the songs and banners and coats of arms of chivalry. No longer the confrontation of adversary knights or armies. But the button switch. As clean as efficient as a river inundating a valley. So the fire drake of flame from streams of planes. The Grendel belching and the monster rearing. In one and myriad pyrotechnic horror of display. Displaying death. In a tournament which deafens and defeats itself for winning. Since the victim disappears. In total victory of the victor. Who or which annihilates and retreats from the siege-field. All nullified by total-destruct. No booty left behind for pillage and remembrance of success and heroics.

Today there are no heros. Only victors. No victims. Mostly death. The neuter symbols of a glory we don't shout about. In compulsion to destroy life. Not return it with conditions. To the souls who've lost the battle. So the whole grim gesture. Won't allow us either to retreat or advance. We live suspended rather. Catching our breath sharply. Grey faced and haunted by death which leaves us cold. Indifferent to it as we are to numbers we cannot add subtract divide or multiply. So infinite and repetitious. Like machines we feed with problems we have made. But cannot solve. Ourselves the victims of our own creations. That feed us breakdowns of our selves and souls. The shreds of abstruse forms and modulations of the spirit. Lost to number and infinity. Immortalized and banked. Computerized in systems of themselves. The saints of new religions. Fed by wires. Cables. Transistors. Assemblies of machines and laser beams. Hierarchies unto themselves. All interdenominational in the void of sound and digit. As they interplay their structures in the chant of test scores scored and meshing in their wires of command. Each socket and each nodule. Endless in their mass of hierophant obedience and command moduled to score. Always to score.

Our technology is always to score. The win is based on volume. On structure and super-structure. Matter matters. And creates matter. But un-like soul. It has no outlet except more matter. Matter is never invisible. But accumulative. It is indigestible. But must be used. Consumed. It pollutes us with the detritus of itself which never serves us any thing but itself in kind. It never transforms only transfers. Like the barter it is. In kind for kind. Commerce. Traffic. Pander and Prostitution. Schemes and Deals. Mergers. And Wagers. Bluffs and Braggadocios. *Faites vos jeux*. To game. To hunt. To hound and harry. To corner the victim. To surfeit us all.

NINE

A SURFEIT OF THE land.
As wished for. Seeking.
All the old nobility. Of choice. For favor.
In the long sleep. Haunted. By the long days dying. In the chosen. Of the few commandments. Ruminant. Like masticating cattle. Horses chawing in the bit. The silence driven. And the grasses stirring in the wind of steppes. Where grain and fodder. And the cactus. And the palo verde. And the mesquite. And the tamarisk in purple plumes. And rattlers like sentinels of hate and fear. Lash out their venom. If disturbed. Lie idly otherwise. In long and lingering aestivations. Under shadow stone. And sleep between their growth. And gatherings of food.

So stands the long and barren history of our "bayonetted plains." The *Llano Estacado*. Where the

Spaniards left their braggadocio of fear and flight. In the cruelty behind. Forever jesting with their own conflicting legends. Of faith fanaticized. Demanding that their stamp of surety and possession. Be branded into history and the ways of man. And time and change. Which never wants to change. Like the vast estancias. In their grim embrace and visor grip. Of ownership of meat and wool on the hoof. Burning into the withers of their kind. The "T Bar O" or "XYZ" or "7 Star Q" or any other spread of earth and blood-bath holding. That symbolizes its proud owner grant of permit. To deliver. And inherit in descent of kind. In festoons and in garlands. Far and wide across the plains. The sharp bit daggers that will gnaw the flesh. And draw the blood of cattle and of man. In wires barbed. That barb.

So this is entry. And inheritance of land. The "I came here first." Which. In the passions of the flesh. In angers of the times gone wild. Where rages reigned in blaze and gory glory. In ten bit saloons and grubstake holdings. Where the sourdough lorded his scrubby scrofulous command. On the tinker wagon called the "chuck." Which dished out all the stuffings. In the bellies of desperate men. Abandoned to wind and weather. To the heat and cold and wind and dust. And the apache and his red-skinned enemies and brothers in vengeance on the paleface who starved them out of food and precipiced the buffalo to death and ambushed the lordly eagles. So that plumes and hides were rare. Instead of nature's surfeit. No longer lavish as before.

Before when?
Before. The time when man like animal. Was nomad. Wanderer. Like minstrel. Fanning out in bands. His groups and clans. Fixed in patterns of the weather. Like clouds that form and disappear. And merge and change. With weather. And the climate. With the stars. The moon. The setting and the rising sun. With seasons of the spirit. Of the body. Of the mind. Moving on the reflex instincts. Noble in the nature of the gesture needed. To survive meant not to hoard beyond the belly's need. So that provisions for the spirit were just as meaningful. The tendon of the buffalo. Its meat scraped clean to feed. Could now be tendered lovingly. With awe. As man in spirit lavishing his love and deep respect. For brother buffalo or bear. Or as among the fisher folk. Their long far distant brothers. The Kwakiutl. In their blood and brother clans of salmon, beaver, whale. And Sasquatch. Friendly hoary hairy spirit of the forest. Rich hoard sources of the potlatch. The cedar groves in vast and giant sentinels of majesty and command. Immortal species immortal spirit. Immortalized in Skeena and in other totems. By mortal man. Who seeks remembrance and regeneration in what nature makes and forms. Where man will re-produce. As best he can. The form of nature. In a form

of man. Where nature triumphs. Even in the art of separation in the form of mask or totem or of fetish. Because the creature man who made it. Doesn't separate the creature from the man. The self from the inspiration of the source. Are still as one. Triumphant. In the dual spirit rendered. Not divided and in conflict. As is modern man. But dual in the oneness of the spirit rendered. Partaking of each other's source of life. And being. In the full and ripening symbol. Of the emblem which it represents. And is.

So the Hopis. The people of the Southwest *Llano Estacado* Plains. Berthed in the rebirth of the lonely buttes. That form the shadows of the sun. And wide expanses of the sky. Their dome of blue. In pearl and silver cloud. And blazing pomegranate sunsets. Purpling their glow to black before the darkness. The light of burning glow and sombre dark. Suspended in a hot and cold. In their color contrasts joined as well.

The Hopis will tell you of their struggle. In this their Fourth World. To emerge. As spirit of the good in man. After all the wanderings in 4 directions: north south east and west. After all the tablets. As in Moses fashion like the Hebrews. Theirs bequeathed to them. Their maze of magicked symbols: "corn cloud, sun, moon, star, water, snake, *nakwách*, (symbol of brotherhood) spirit of the creator, and bear tracks." In the power and prayer and purification. Which the wanderings invoked. To fulfill the Creator. In His Creation of Mankind. In them His people. In their Fourth World struggle. As the chosen people. In their sustenance to succeed. On the plateau of aridity. Antelope Mesa: Awatovi (Place of the Bow). First Mesa: Walpi (The Gap). Sichomovi (Flower Mound). Hano (The People). Polacca. Second Mesa: Mishongnovi (Rising Up Place). Shungopovi (Tall Weeds by the Spring Village). Shipaulovi (Where the Mosquitos Are). Third Mesa: Oraibi (Where the Orai Rock Is). Moenkopi (By the Running Water). Kiakochomovi (Hill of Ruins) or New Oraibi. Hotavila (The Place of a Spring Inside a Cave Where a Low Entrance Might Scratch Your Back). Bacabi (Place of the Reeds). Between the Colorado. And the Rio Grande. Where before. In all three worlds. Of wandering and confusion and impurity. They had failed.

TEN

TRAGEDY IS HEROISM without end.
For if it stops. Then comedy ensues.
As we would like. In our predilections.
To form plots. And forms. And tell a story in the confines of our bounds of chance. Which humanly we would predict as best we can. And so we feel a formulaic pattern of repose. Relieved by sighs of satisfaction. Like the belch. Or even the erection. Fruition in coition. Even bowel movements. Have an end as well as a beginning. So like the clowns we are or would be. We would have comedy forever. In the theatrics of our own distractions. We would never circumscribe or call a halt to. Because the tensions of the mysteries. Of fate. The wheel that never stops to call the number. The wheel that never stops to make decrees. And to extract both payment and reward. Is better in a limbo of its own. A circle perfect without end and/or beginning. Never seen in any number of the parts. To enthrall or frighten us. With

palpitations of our own dead reckoning. Because it's better to have played. Than won or lost. As also with the comedy of our lives. Without any wagers or commitments. Just play for play. The seesaw in the sand pile. The child in man or woman. Seething for fulfillment in a non-fulfilling meaninglessness. Joy without end. And "so they lived." "Happily ever after."

As so all story. With its limitation. Wantonly to effect. The intimacy of a kiss. Where those who truly love. Prefer to love without the sharing. Because it limits the depth and breadth and possibilities. It wants to be. To flourish in an all. Consuming no one in particular or any thing. Just giving of itself in all directions. In all directions. Without a compass. Without end. Floundering when it wants to. Retreating and advancing. As some tidal wave of mystery without causality. Existencing in its own extension. A force of nature. Within the nature of the nature of itself. Within man.

So comedy is all our dreams of life come true. And not the life. Where tragedy is what we would avoid. Insisting that it surely not. Must not exist. Refusing to give sustenance to its substance. Because like hunger that's grown monstrous. Tragedy refuses recognition of its limitations. As if it had any in the mind of man. For like man himself. Tragedy must find co-existence with the ego. Which seeks its being in fulfillment without end. Refusing definition. Other than the mystery of the mystery of itself. Eternally demanding. In an eternity without end.

A people must find form in one or other. Of either comedy or tragedy. To be American you see is still a comedy. A game of make believe we are the people of our dreams. But if our dreams are only dreams. And never touch upon reality. We'll never seek foundations. In a mystery of our own extensions. Only play the game of professing to be real and true and good. Always peering cautiously behind the masque of being. Going to the ball. Which never ends.

So with our entertainments. Our *entre-meses.* Our delectations. Tease and starve our substance craving to be fed. Appeased by blood and vengeance. Spirit will and soul. Like other individuals of myths and spirits of peoples and of nations and of civilizations. The Job or Oedipus Tyrannus. King Arthur Lear Quixote. Socrates Joan of Arc. And their kind. We'll never know heroism. Because in spirit and in substance of what we believe. In practice of our credo of circumspection. Our common sense is our shield and coat of mail. Cancelling battles and struggles. Robbing us of discomforts. As unbecoming a people of an indigenous empire. Colonial from its very beginnings.

We are an island of cruelty unto ourselves. Our largesse our bounty. Is the largesse the bounty of our girth our spread. Like Gulliver amongst the Lilliputians. We are gigantic. And cannot feel our surroundings. So miniscule is feeling compared to power.

Why feel when we can command. So we order our lives with the comedy of rhetoric. And occasionally we grieve and grope aimlessly on the tightrope of our circus enclosures of the mind. As we applaud ourselves but wonder as we wander in distraction of our own imposing. Why we tire of the surfeit of our force and grandeur. Eating cakes and ices. When we desire bread and cheese.

Bread and cheese. And ashheaps and shards. And boils and blisters. And fevers. And visions. And leprosy. And hemlock. And barren heaths. And burnings at the stake. And Excaliburs in stone. And burning bushes. And waters parted. And voices out of the whirlwind. And oracles at Corinth or at Thebes. Or anywhere. Fighting windmills for giants. All these and more. And many more. As Sisyphus rolling his stone. Or Everyman carrying his burden. Or Christian trudging thru his Slough of Despond. Are all there behind and before us. Without end. But we are a people of short memories and strengths. And cannot endure. Even though we wish to prevail.

To endure is not always to prevail.
To endure is to endure even when we know we're losing or might lose. It means to fight with grace and spirit. And more often without force.

But we Americans are people of force.
We cannot face endurance. The substance of struggle is not for us to anguish over. No forms no ceremonies. The business of dying is a business an affair. Not a confrontation human and divine.

War for us is everywhere. A meeting with force against force. Matter versus matter. Never or rarely spirit versus spirit. Tragedy is spirit allowing itself to be seen felt suffering exposed. Even our tragedies are comedies. They rise and descend from matter. Always expendable.

As recently as yesterday. We tried to feel a tragedy. Souls rent from body. In our limbs from matter. Torn on the bark. Of pain we cannot feel. In our forest of suicide. Of spirit arrested. And self inflicted. Bypassing feeling. Like an aorta valve. Losing its blood and its life beat. Sickened and dying.

We try to resurrect ourselves. Dazed and deadened. From being self-mesmerized. Pretending death is unimportant. Tragedy is unimportant. Feeling is unimportant. Only principle idea and form. Only the comedy of life as farce.

As when prisoners and their hostage guards are sacrificed as numbers. Not as souls. Expedient to the greater evil of loss of face and principle. As law and order emerges. Bloodless and triumphant. But after the blood the sacrifice. Like Pilate or Lady Macbeth. Or any king usurper. We cannot wash away the blood. Or even close the gap of credibility. The more we wash away or try or theorize or rationalize. The less we say we feel but know we're right. The more we pile the guilt upon ourselves. The less we are believed.

The tragedy at a prison called Attica. Where the governor of a state comports himself like a ghoul from some region of the undead. Telling all of us that death is nothing but a casualty. Expendable to principle. To law and order. That victims of man. Are victims. Not souls. Whereas death without man's cold ego bungling of bureaucracy and force in action. Was always death confronting spirit. But the crushing of the prison rebellion at Attica this past week. Will never be retrieved from farce. We'll never know to judge it as a cry of anguish and of anger. Where souls of beings died. Just felons. Enemies to principle. Figures that must be erased. And were. Like digits that will never be accounted for. So many debits in the way of the books and scales of Justice. Aptly symbolized as blinded. To be objective. Is not to see or feel. It is easier to succeed that way. And we are a people of efficiency. We always invariably succeed.

ELEVEN

NOT TO PAUSE by.
In the nature of the flowering. The flower
of that which is. Confides to you and others and myself.
The self which seeks and savors in its own search find-
ings.

Not that always we can prove renewal.
The substance of the thing we call ourselves. At any given moment. Seeks to flee. The vanish
is a mute asseveration. Of the difficulty in the unknown.
To be seized upon and known.

Here am I. The writer of the long day's
journey into night. The dawns and sunsets of my trials
and errors. Coloring and shadowing. Advances hesita-
tions and retreats. The all grim shadow play of day's

renewal into Time and Age. The sum and substance hover of a moment's seizure into sure full certainty. Before the burst that blooms it disappears. In never to be remembered or recorded recognition.

So thus we try.
Our own true thrust.
Which sometimes in the loss of gains.
Withdraws in shy and grim discourage-
ment.

The scenes. The silences. The struggles. To seize upon reality. And make it fully as your own. Where forests of the soul. The chambered nautilus. In oceans of the spirit's surge. That hums reverberation into all that elevates and bends you to the grovel knucklings of the clenched fist. And the burning tears. Where. As in other poet thinker Emersons of past insurgency. "All mean egotism vanishes."

Transparent eyeballs and the like. Or other ways to try perception. Of something other than the self that moves. Impulsion and compulsion. All as different or as one. "The force that thru the green fuse drives the flower." Into substance of our own true reckoning. All this and more. We strive and forage. Like the beetle or the slug or nematode or caterpillar. Grub or mealy bug. Borer. Earwig. Coddling moth. Aphid. Whitefly. Thrip. Or mite. Parasite is parricide. The generation into life and substance all your own. Is death upon the thing that feeds you.

How vulture-like is man. The garbage of the matter of his dreams' inventions. Scuttling like a crab or monster chiton. In his armor. Over seas of air and water. In the oceanic universe of planetary full decomposition.

Where then can all his placements and pronouncements lead him. But to end his time and moment. Where the full possession glory of some small discovery. Thrills him to no end. Except for sustenance of private faith and prayer. Where others would deny the very genuflection of the knee. Or laying on of hands. For blessings and full recognitions of the spirit hovering. The way a hummingbird will dance its full suspension. In a seizure of the substance of some flower. In the vine or tree or bush. That furnishes its food.

Like soul gatherers.
Like food gatherers.

Like all of man's civility in cultures of his own production. Which we call human histories of time and fate. Necessity though blind. Which drives us to our doom. As biologic with the life that breathes. Our full suspension in extension of ourselves. Seals silent parchments. In our hungers of the moment's needs. And wings us to our transitory victories. Or anguishing and long defeats.

So we Americans.
Of this our seventh decade. In the century some said we would invent. And stamp with our patent of the surety of our sense of know-how.

We always have. In our brief and brawling days of past destruction. Known what to do. And how to do it. Whether we should have done. What we have done. Is another matter for someone who is not American to decide.

We would crush cultures. The ethnic eccentricities of our past. The wearying return of vibes we all can recognize. American as we are. Homeric in our embryonic seething broils. Parades and catalogs of peoples places and their struggles and their fates. The same. The same. In weary repetition of their fates. No different than our parents and our own. Who came before the struggles of our sisters and our brothers and our children. Anglo Scotch Irish Italian Jewish Nordic Slavic Black Puerto Rican Chicano. And the stranger enemy. The "arab" of the buffalo plains. The mountains. And the sea. Our nomad ghost. Algonkian or Sioux. Cheyenne. Apache. Ute. Hopi. Esquimau. The mongol tartar non-caucasian redskin. Of our territory. That was formerly his.

Always. In the same thrust. Crushing every eccentricity and dream ascension. That would keep chords umbilical alive. Or languages with strange astounding thrusts. Each nuance like a ritual of dissonant reverberation. Apartheid in some dialect of song and story. That recorded heroisms from another land and time. Where on other continents. Beginnings of traditions rose and fell. And fought. Enduring to the end of time. Like melodies of songs forgotten. That linger in some fright of memory. That ghosts before your vision. Now and then.

So we. As attitudes. Renew ourselves. And find oblivion. And self-denial. Our true asseveration of some kind. Where difference crushes difference. And blanches memories. And stifles murmurings of prayers and curses and caresses in other tongues. To dominate in anglo pidgin English of American. My brother. My compatriot. My enemy. My friend. My own. My kind.

TWELVE

ACCEPTANCE IS THE BETTER part of valour.

This is not to say we live in compromise.

The artist is an animal apart. Who ages like his kind. The biologic fluid in his veins. Will beat like metronomes. To the music and the pattern of his beat. Which scores and doesn't score. Depending on the tremors of assurance or hesitation. The sweating hands. The sweat upon the forehead. The round. The square. The triangle. All multiplied in the angle of the vision. Gesture and defiance from within. Which shafts you to the very marrow of your angered bones. Reactionary to the times you live in.

That this is so is not some new idea of course. To hate and scrounge into your corner of concealment. Gnashing teeth and lip and knuckle and nail.

Balanced on the prayer you would believe in and defend. To your dying breath of life. Yes. This is so. There is no other recourse but acceptance. That position of your way. Is yours and yours alone. To fight for and defend. If you are flushed by quarry of your enemy. There you are. Defenseless and alone.

So such is harrowing. For soldier and for farmer as for artist. You must defend the soil you've conquered or you've nurtured. Either one or both. It's all the same. Perfection is the preparation from the lifetime's seeding or of feeding.

Embracing all your territory conquered. In a thrust of will. You are embattled as the farmer soldier. That stood his ground on Concord Bridge. Or Hastings. Shrewsbury. Or Agincourt. This all true history. Of this your life's reach. A heroism blind and hidden. In the secrets nurtured for protection. And for life. It's life you would defend. Against the odds of death. That lies around you. That you must live through and endure. To keep alive. And feel alive. And be alive.

Balzac cried against and all about it. Death and taxes wasn't it he said and so repeated. Thus these our full responsibilities of territories won. The properties of sweat. We would endure and fight for. To enclose our spirit in a solitude. That borders on exhaustion. That precious silence and full privacy of spirit. Which we earn by fighting in our vassalage. To taxes and to property. To bring life forth from death of spirit. Which we recognize in doing all the work that is the world's. And not our own.

      So feudalism therefore is not over.

      It's like the fate that shows itself. Suspended like a spider's web. Upon our lives. We toil and labor in the beauty of its form. But must be careful not to catch ourselves. Instead of willing and unwilling victims. In its web. A creation fully. And as long forever is. Our own.

      The poet then's. No different from the Viking. Brandishing his spirit. Like the thunderous surge of sea upon the longboats. In the estuaries and the fens and bogs. In around the islands. And the bastions. Pirating in stealth. The hours of his time and moment. Waiting. As the hammer to the anvil. To strike and make the sparks fly. In a victory or even a defeat. That sings out gloriously.

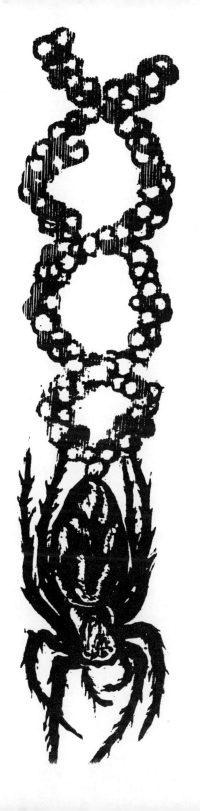

Thus hatred. In the wars of passion and vendetta. The barons in the Norman duchies. In their thrust for fame. As fearful of themselves. Of one another. As fear can be. But striking deadly and in callous pride. One and then another. As young Duke William knew. The bastard son of Robert scion of Hrolf. Who fevered in the quartan sickness. On his pilgrimage's return from salvation in Jerusalem. Bequeathed his son of seven. The frights and fights of struggle for succession and protection of property and power. Seized and won.

Thus we must. If chosen. In the fate that knows no compromise. Strike quickly. Or be stricken. Or be touched by fate itself. Which prepares us for the struggle to stay alive. Just barely. By the skin of our teeth. Hiding. And surviving. Like the needle in the haystack. For William then. The hours of the fates. Of Time's scythe. Struck down men. His own protectors and sustainers. Like wheat in the field. Mowed down. First Alan of Brittany poisoned. Then guardian Gilbert of Brionne in cold blood. Then Thurold his tutor murdered. The horror of the drama. The drama of the horror. All life. All history. Reality in supernatural coloration. Gigantic in its frightful truth. As truth can sometimes be. But rarely is. At Vaudreuil Castle next. Island-berthed in the river Eure. Young Duke William slept. A Moses in the bulrushes. While frogs croaked in the reeds outside. Assassins slew the seneschal Osbern Crépin. Groped for his ward William. Saved "in the nick of time."

The soldier of fate and fortune. Mailed or exposed. With pen or with sword. If chosen. Excalibur is real. And so is Grendel. Cross or dragon. The burden is the burden. Before the enemy. The death we would deny. While inching towards it. As all a part of struggle. In the life that is. The battle stations posted to us. Dispatching us to them. With all due speed. As we awake. In the midstream. The midnight. The mid-watch. Of our lives. And realize in the sweat and angst of the moment. That it is ours. For us to do battle. In the cause we've lotteried and fought for. And it is now or never. As it ever or never was before.

THIRTEEN

WHERE THEN TO VICTORY for sure. Is not a portion of the way as cast for destiny. For time which ripens to the way. As path for cover. Of protection gains. Returns the moment to its tidal wave. And we as won. To find ourselves alone. For victory returns the victor to his spoils.

Why. And as for sure. Command. As legions of the Romans. Or of Pyrrhus. Bent upon the gain. For profit taking. Not for profit sharing. Or by William Conqueror. Son of Robert the Magnificent. Nephew to that Uncle enemy Geoffrey the Hammer. And vassal to the King who succored him awhile. Henry who became alarmed because the weakling underdog. Became the overlord. Inspiring fear and horror and surrender. In his wholesale severing of arms and feet. Because the rallying point of energetic flame and full rebellion of those Norman new-born generations of sons of fathers. Barons and Dukes. And overlords themselves. Who conquered and destroyed. And re-aligned again. To fire and starve and siege. And played the game of chess. Of history's feverish territorial spread and sprawl. Where land and state and property. Were rallying banners. To regroup and plunder. Winter Summer Spring and Fall. In the undulating valleys where the rivers surged and dipped their full fertility upon the land of Normandy. The strawberries and poppies wild in splendor. Trampled by the horses and their mounts. And armor clanging. As the metal and the flesh of horse and man. Dripped blood upon the land. And gorged the rivers with the drowning fleeing ghosts of rebels cowed and fleeing. The victories of Val-ès-Dunes and Arques. Defeating Ralph the Badger. Haimo the Toothy. Rebel William against rebels Guy of Burgundy. Rannulf and Niegel of the Cotentin.

Ambitious William had his singers. Wace. And William of Poitiers. As Homer sang. Of the Achaians. And the Trojans. In a far remoter time. When the Mycenaeans thrust their pressures. And their energies. Upon the guardians of the Hellespont. And crushed the "generous Troad." And pirated and plundered. Through the Phrygia Mysia. The Sea of Marmara Propontis. Byzantium and Chalcedon. Beside the Bosporus. Into the Pontus Euxinus. Of what we call the Black Sea of today.

So all we call ambition. The epic and the saga of the destinies of men. Are accidents of birth and time and place. The situation calling for a thrust of energy and horror. Deceiving both the victim and the victor. Where those who win are never in the field. Where blood and grime are. And where life ends for some. And begins for others.

The winners. Are like Pyrrhus in their victories. Manipulating destiny to gain. Where epic elevation is reduced to human slaughter. And to momentary changes of the scene. Where those who won before. Become the losers. Where the former losers now become the victors.

And so it goes. This seesaw gift of history. They call nationhood and manifest destiny.

Onward and upward. Downward and Eastward and Westward. And Northward and Southward. Until one day Time stops. Because there'll be an end. To where it goes from here to there. Because there'll no longer be a here or there or anywhere. To go to or to come from.

As for sure.
The day and moment.
Of a hero's trial.
Is not always. That of spirit moving. But an impetus. To seek for. As to win. To try and sever. All that comes your way. In ultimate of ways for sure. Which never are. As sure as fortune made them. Or so you think. And find it otherwise. Because. Impelled. As so you are. To do and serve. The that which moves you to the life as lived. The spirit of your trials and errors. Like the game of sport. Of boxing. Or of tennis. Or of skiing. Or of swimming. Or of climbing mountains. Or racing on your racing cycle. All of sport. Or art. Are both and one the same. In the exhilaration of the energy expended.

But art is somewhat more. Than being different from the sport of energy expended. While this it is. Additionally. It's more. As of the magic of its seed of conquest made. The thing produced. The product of an energy expended. And a spirit formed. It lives in others. In the life it makes. In full transmission of the gift and benediction of its kind. Like seed and flour and bread. It germinates and breeds. And multiplies. The yeast of spores of generations of its fermentation. In continuum. Where unlike progress. Art makes no incision on the mightier. Than thou. Or I. Or them. But moves in time and change. And fleshes into fruit. And is consumed without destruction. Of itself or others.

Only matter destroys matter. Never art. Which lives a history apart from progress. In the history of matter's evolution. And corruption. And dissolution.

That which feeds. And never seeks to covet. Because it is of spirit. In essence of its manifest of form. Though form is of the matter of its own full substance. It is not of the essence of the matter of its substance. But of the spirit of the substance. From which it springs. The art.

FOURTEEN

THE RHYTHM OF EACH repetitious act.

As writing without thoughts. To guide by. Or to lead. To others new. And scenes. As actions of the drama recreated. For the moment. As the curtain raiser. To a new beginning. As a substance of some plot or form. Seeks shapes of human being. To perform.

With as the wherewithal. To find. The passion feeding on itself. To form. As story rides the book. The hour. And the page. The life style. That tells parables of morality. So formed. That wrested. From our silent dissolutions. We would return to blood and kin and kind. Declaring it in all its blind deception. To be thicker than the water. Of the riverun. The one that comes thru taps. In city and suburban sinks. And rural wells. That pump the lime and all the other phosphate minerals and salts. Where drink is seepage. Earthy as the age of geologic core. The silt of centuries and eons of the sweats and vapors. And the dews of ageless mornings. And their mists. And evenings of evaporations. From the sun. In all its glorious days of burning. Baking baking baking. Into ovens of earth.

How try. To wither. As the core denied. The single simple gesture of belief. That family nation priest and plague. Are superstition's links to fate and destiny. And place. And moment. On the edge of time. As space suspended in the spirit. Must seek to make incisions on our mind. And force us to decisions of belief. As if the world were rational withal. And society. And social custom. Were the forms of norms. To rally our behaviour. That we would call human. And not just forms of norms as such.

As when whoever said and proved. That literature. To be itself. Must be a story. Or that life of someone. That was once a fetus. Must take family. To remain alive. Community. Of thee I sing. And hate its forms that smother and that suffocate. The reason being of the self. That wishes neither to destroy or lie. But just give vent to fullness. To allow of growth. To feed upon the air that wishes us to live the life we've made.

Without which. Selfishness. And again desire. Affords us. In the spirit of the flesh. To sing. To breathe. And suppurate the pores. The lesions. And the healing after. As the flower of the bloom on trees. That bud. In burst of narrow space and pressure. In the sun warmed dawns. And autumn earth of summer heat and sleep. Which feeds and berths the roots in winter sleep. So soul of vegetable. Or of human not divine. Seeks spirit. In the stretch of life. To form. And thus. To reach its character of kind. Refuses in its struggle toward creation. To seek all form. In stunted retrogression.

We must not be the victims of repression. Of the social. Or the fable kind. That seeks to place you. By your label color tongue blood and form. In a race apart from singularity. Of spirit. Or of soul. To clan you. In a vise of grim and gross beliefs and ways. And attitudes apartheid. Which blood suck into the marrow of your veins. And make your spirit shake with fear. Until retreat into those others and their ways. Becomes your bottom dollar. To invade you and take over. So that you and yours belong to something called a race a people. And the scrimshaw of their patterns of belief. Will set like voodoo in your blood. And make you quake and shiver. Laugh and cry and hate. And suffer others to enjoy. The punishment you've chosen. In their love of you they say. Which selfishly denies the sharing. Of anything against them. Or apart.

So thus does Western man. Renounce the pattern of humanity. For being human in himself. He bleeds. And worships in the blood what is familiar. And erects his Stonehenge. His magic circle of the clan and seasons. And the cult. And stays within it. And makes the laws to keep himself his own blood prisoner. In the lineage he calls his family and his race.

As man is mythic making. So the lies are true. The opposite of the forms they breed. To hide our true beliefs and cruelties. And loves and fears. Because we would be family and society. And be the winner in the numbers we belong to. That makes clan race government. Erasing our particulars. In worn out genes. That reproduce themselves. And so we worship repetition in the dominant strain of our species. And sometimes wonder why we're bored with that we've chose to worship. Because of its familiarity.

They sometimes say. Familiarity breeds contempt. But proof points otherwise. To self-satisfaction. Found in those who act alike. Because they do not think. Or if they do. Agree. Without the actuality of a thought. That seeks ingestion. Or rejection.

As thus to futures. For societies to serve. Depends on life. And possibility. And soul. And spirit. Where an individual is forced to feel rejection. When he must follow new direction. For the essence of the life. The soul. The spirit. The voice. The urge. The destined self-direction. He or she is forced to follow. And to feel. In irony and paradox. Renews the clan. Which is a lie and fable to the truth of human substance. In form and new direction. A revolution-evolution. And denial of the past and present. For a future waiting and all new.

FIFTEEN

HER ON THYSSUN GEARE *waes se mycla hungor geond.* Was said in the *A.S.C.* Of the year 1005. But any year or time of any people. Might be the same. To state the difference from the year before. Of plenty. *Mycla.* To be had. Of food. To *hungor geond.* The famine that was then throughout. In *Angel land.*

Swa grimme it was. So grim it is today. The hunger. The famine bleeding us. Our veins of rich returns upon our stock in trade and holdings. Fat cat banks in Switzerland. In concrete without windows. Are the vaults. The resonance of hoards. That sentence death. To victims that would live their lives in peace. Or in forgetfulness. Instead. Upon the grimy battle lines. Battalions. Like far-distant legions of the Romans. Past centuries ago. Posted to the battles of defeat. Where ignominy reigns in hot and sweaty jungle growth. Encircled by the stench of powder. After blasts have blown some sorry flesh to death. And souls of memories of the living. Parted in forever of finality. To lie bleeding and unknown. Unmourned by those who do not understand. That jungles in a land of Stone Age man. In Southeast Asia. Are front-lines for defence from fear. And fear's attack. In a village of Ohio. Or of Maine. Or Indiana. Or Louisiana. Or perma-frosted Yukon. And Alaska. So the *unknown soldier* of Hill "C" or "D." That was shattered to smithereens. On some bright sunny day. Or early morning. Yawning lazily and innocent. Or tense and overdrawn from watchful knowing. And from weariness beyond his years. Dies suddenly and swiftly. In his battle of Thermopylae. Or Marathon. Or Plataea. Or if we would Homeric him. Like some one of Priam's 50 sons. Defending his position beneath the thickness of some jungle overgrowth of vines. As they behind before against the walls of Troy. Or at the river of Scamander. Or by the sea.

So we beside ourselves. Sit vigil. Set by needs not ours. But told they'd better be. Defending and promoting our G N P. Our *Iliad* of the hour. Only the rich can sing about. Accompanying our minstrel poets of the government-apple-pie and mother and father-land-nationhood game. As they jounce and jingle and whine. Rattling their sabers. Clashing their wills. Screetching commands. Vollying bombs and machinery and missiles. In threats and sallies. And thrusts of verbal harangue. Promising to defend the peace. By imitating war.

And so a famine reigns. This year of lean returns and tightening of the stomach muscles. As we grind to a halt. In anger and reprisal. Of our hates and frustrations. No marches. No bombings. No barricades stateside. No political theaters of street ambushes. No deaths of innocents in mobs of student protests. Defenceless and truculent. As waves of spirit in idealism. Try and fail. Unlike Moses. To part the waters. And fall. As gently. And as finally. As flowers in the field. No more of all these screams and wailings. On the wailing wall that is our country. All of it. Its beauty. And its promise. And its space. Its fertility of welcome. In our centuries of celebration and thanksgiving. Where every man and woman and their offspring. Buried their ghosts of history and oppression. Clan against clan. And hid from armies of the Czar. And ran across the barren tundras. The Siberias. And the desert drought and dust and listless heat of southern Sicilies. And humid humorless northern rains and stubborn craggy soil. That seeded nothing but the famine of the potato. And all these came. And more. And dreamed. And struggled. Huddled in the dank dark warrens. Stinking of olive oil and matzoh balls and garlic and cabbage and corned beef and stews of tripe and rotted horsemeat. Huddled like ancient paleolithic man in his cave. As they in theirs. Warming their spirits and their bodies. On coal stoves and alcohol burners. And humbly. Like tattered exiled kings. Lifting their weary bodies above the grime. The privation. Singing anthems of praise. For the privilege of denial of all the riches of tradition and fable and romance and history and above all tyranny that was theirs. For this new freedom of struggle. Where man as primitive. Must grovel and fight. And take punishment. And eat dust. And live in detritus. But hold his head high. Because there was the dream. And this gave him room to rise. And the famine of the body. Never touched the dream of his spirit. And though the pavements of the New World were not as he dreamed. Paved in the stones of Eldorado. It was sufficient for him to believe in the dream. His spirit insisted was true. Who can argue with Don Quixote or Candide's mentor. Pangloss. That all's for the best. In this best of all possible worlds?

SIXTEEN

AMERICA IS PROMISES. They once did say. From the mountain. To the prairie. The promise of the seizure of a dream. As sworn to dedication. As rebellion from the nightmare of some past. To rebellion for the cause. As individual. As the kinds and sects and countries. Where the vengeance. Was a vengeance on the past. As sometimes only. Just because it was the past. A symbol of rebellion for a child.

But countries are like families. In the mold and substance. Of the forms they breathe. And breed upon. And if the earth and air and spores of life. Deny the past. The pattern of the seed. And genus of the species. Will then respond another way to yours. Oh European. And so American becomes what it becomes. Because we want to. Or we willed it. Whether we still want. What we willed. When we arrived. Is another matter still. The one we haven't come to terms with. In the way of child or rebel. That we were. And are. As still we probe and probe ourselves to death. And even after we have died we don't find heaven. Even then. As well as not before.

And so it goes. So hard core. So we boast and bet our bottom dollar. As we seek. And hardly ever find. That mythical rainbow. In the Eldorado of our dreams. Oh yes we dream. And never call the dream a nightmare. Because we are a topsy-turvy people. Gulliverian and Alice-In-Wonderland. The child-in-adult who builds Disneylands and Hollywoods. To perpetuate the dream. Of all that future that is blatant with success. As we sing our odes and benedictions to our many gods. All new and shiny in their artificial molds. The pepper-upper. And the pill to sleep. The mouth breath freshener. And the underarm deodorant. The shampoo that doesn't fib its dye. The un-cola. And our degermed cereals and breads and cakes. But we can limp to health with the vitamin bottle. And chase away the pressure and the pain. With aspirin or mary jane. Or any other weed that serves the same. To turn us more and more away from smells and tastes and death-in-age. And all that's natural and dependent and fatal. Delusion is the better part of valor for us. The glamor we would war for. And bleed ourselves to death. In taxes that define our property. And the elevated status we support.

Our G N P is then our Zeus. The pantheon of profit we've erected. Not bad for a people without a past. Or when they give some small community its head. For maybe several generations. Like New York's Washington Square. Or San Francisco. Our Rome of many hills. Or all the adobe Spanish Mexican Indian towns and villages and squares and churches and missions. Sooner or later they will be either razed or antiqued. Antiqued and preserved and improved. To create what is known as a past. We never fully had. And only now imagine. Or razed. For the present which is our future. And never truly the present. Because a present is a present. By distinction from the past. But we are an unusual genus or species. We create a present. To live in the future.

To live in the future. Means never to rest. Even though we feel tired and confused. And at this moment. We do feel tired and confused.

But the role of the rebel child is ours of our own choice. And never admits defeat. And therefore doesn't rest. And plays games and games. And dreams dreams. And creates nightmares of industry and pollution. And jousts with wheelers and dealers. Tycoons and Robber Barons. And Bushwackers of real estate. And if you're not happy says the child to himself. Always be envious. And never take the blame. Take any joy enjoyed by others. Away from others. No one in America has a right to be different. Our right our duty our fate. Is everywhere and all. Every last one of us. To be the same.

Once it was unity in diversity. When we still remembered what our fathers and mothers remembered. Snatches of Liszt's Hungarian Rhapsodies and a little Hungarian. And grandmother's tales. Of how she was snatched by the gypsies. Spirited away for awhile. And then returned. In the cold clean stony ordered elegance. Of the Esterhazy castle. In the old country. Still old. And still Esterhazy. And still Austria. But not the Empire. Grandmother left behind. An aristocrat. Americanized through struggle. And hope of what? Freedom. Independence. Berthing 8 sons and 1 daughter. And making sauerkraut and wine and bread and cake and goulash and pastries. And rising at 4. Or before dawn. To feast us all thru the weekends of families and friends and internecine quarrels and temporary "let's be friends again" Cousin or Aunt or Uncle or Nephew or Niece. The turbulence. And the welcomes and departures. And the operas in their arias sung. And the jazz. And the blues. Played and sung. And the stand-up comedians and the ethnic improvisations. It was a moment when you weren't allowed to be unhappy. Because you knew you still belonged. Even if the belonging became later. Like anything we prefer to destroy. Just because it is tradition. Or just because it's old. Something to be destroyed. And replaced by something new.

SEVENTEEN

To CAST. AS CASTE. Is just as much American.

As Hindu. Or any other form of ritual of status. In a system. Rigid in its artifice of gesture and belief. Morality and politics and religion. The Triune or Triumvirate American. Or Hermes Trismegistus. Thrice-greatest Hermes-Thoth. Egyptian-Greek as One. As Father Son and Holy Ghost. Brahma Vishnu Shiva. Osiris Tammuz/Adonis and Zagreus/Dionysus. Ugaritic Baal. Resurrected by Anath. From Mot. Thus Death and Resurrection. Heaven Earth or Midgard. Hades-Hell. As ritual of human memory and prayer. Repeats its fervency of fear and hope. For Resurrection. After Death-in-Life. Or after-life. Before the heaven or the hell. And after death.

Thus so. As substance of the forms. And ways that make a people. So the dreams repeat themselves. In rituals. As reverberating. As the recent Nazi War Militia. In the trauma of their paranoiac symbol and salute and goose-step march. And swastikas and heils. The nightmare of a time. That no one dreamed was real. Not even Nazis. Who created the nightmare of the reality. That foiled their dream of conquest of the world.

The irony of hate and all its collectivity of belief. Is far more dominant than love. Which for all its general acceptance. Is apartheid and alone. Singular and not collective. Individual and varied. Mysterious. And non-visible. Perceptual. But unseen.

America's trinity is not catholic. But protestant. An ethic of collectivity. That never satisfies. The unfed solitude. Of dreams and hopes and aspirations. Many and varied. As against few and the same.

To be catholic. Is to be universal. To be protestant. Is to rebel. So fitting America. The country of the rebel. Became the country of the protestant. For all.

The country of the elect. Of the common man. Liberty and Equality for all. As long as all your differences of language culture dream. Accepted solubility and anonymity. In the oneness of the ethos of America. Where Mammon became king. Enshrined in the temples of our G N P. Where piety and prosperity. Became our catechism. In the morality of money as the good. And the pure. And the just. And progress and technology. As the fruit of our labor. Our beneficent mass productivity. Blessed and sanctioned by the god of both cartel-corporate entity and union of labor. It's all one and the same. We all want to be rich and protestant and selfish and bigoted. We stand united in the sameness of our goals. And to reach them we all must be the same. We must stand united against the enemy. The one who is different. Who feels different. Who wishes to remain different. And singular. Not plural and collective. The minority versus the majority.

And so the common man. The faceless majority. Who is eternal. The slave. The freedman. The serf. The thegn. The peon. Feudal and abused. And used. Manipulated like the cog he is. On the wheel of Destiny. Of Fortune's Wheel.

In America. He accepts his collectivity. His common nature. He does not see as common. He

sees it as American. And patriotic and moral. "God Bless America." He confuses with the National Anthem. Which no one sings today. Except at funerals in Arlington Cemetery. Or at political rallies and state fairs for the G N P.

On Friday evenings. The end of his week as machinist. In some Porsche or Audi or Ford Assembly Line. Or Repair Shop. He joins another team also competitive. And bowls for General Motors or Ford or Porsche. Or any other priest-sect of the G N P. Establishing his status and acceptance and pride of serfdom. In the vast collective machine he serves. Wearing the shirt of his "team." Not with his name written across the back. But theirs. Satisfaction complete and guaranteed. The serf is loyal to his king. And wears his monarch's standard. Even when his time's his own.

In Pizza Parlors. The tribal gathering place of the common man. The banjo the broken piano. Bang out the songs: "Speak To Me My Melancholy Baby"/"Dixie"/"Che Sera Sera." Ending at midnite with "God Bless America." And the serfs all stand. Proud of their acceptance. And the right to struggle. And pay high taxes. For their suburban 3 bedroom house and bath and a half. And 1 Volkswagon and 1 Datsun. And a power lawnmower and dishwasher and washing machine. And Sear's or Ward's or Penney's bedroom or living-room or both suites. And 3½ children (one in fetus). And guitar and 2 scrambler motorcycle trail bikes. And week-end trailer standing in the street. For all these things. For all these time payments and life and health and accident and house and theft and storm-tornado insurance. Which will perpetuate themselves. The debts of the fathers. Will be visited upon the children. For the privilege of obligations. Their litany of liabilities. Being in debt. Is part of the piety of the system. Everyone expects you to be indebted. If you are not. You can't establish credit or confidence. Mammon G N P. Must have its priesthood of sects. Ford. General Motors. Boeing. Safeway. NBC CBS ABC. Merrill Lynch Pierce Fenner and Smith and their bunch. Kellogg and Campbells Del Monte and Xerox and Shell and Exxon and Texico Consolidated Ma Bell and Edison and so on. And they all practice *limosna*. Asking more and more for their God. And the God of the people. All one. All-powerful. All-American.

EIGHTEEN

"**N**EL MEZZO DEL CAMMIN di nostra vita."

It is not so much being in the middle-half of life. The tribulation and the pain is one of spirit. Not of what the currents biological within. Can do and do. For these are of the seasons and the tidal neap and spring. Which Earth and all its wash of waters oceanic. Periodically. By hour by day by month. By pull of moon and sun. By gravity of law towards or away. By harmony within the law of compensation. Which grotesques the spheres. Related to each other. Earth Moon and Sun. Creating laws of influence. Relative and absolute to us. As one to one. And two to one and two and. As three to three. To one to two and three. To one another.

So we are of the seasons. Solitary. Planetary. Seasonal and seismic. One to one another. As to time. The moment of our given energy. To disperse dispense with. As we can. In this the season of our lives with one another. As with the self. That seems to surge and struggle all alone. Gravitating to its local destination. Struggling yet against its ignorance of self.

Though biologically. The spirit moves as one. With growth and age and blood. And genes and hormones. The self we know. Which disappoints us in the struggle to find the recognition of its own true growth. Occasionally will rise and separate. Suspend itself from its coagulating blood. Its passions tremors and confusions of the moment. And soar perceptively. Like some new logos of a new born elevation. Not of woods and solitudes. Of man or woman. Not of sexuality defined. Or psychological liberation of the ghosts and nightmares from within. But of that neuter noumenon. That postulates itself as self. Related to but separate from masculinity. Or femininity. That says the liberated being does exist. Regardless of disguise in chimpanzee-like biology. Our man-ape world. Which reminds us. Every man and woman offshoot. That we behave as if encaged. Moving in the murky gloom of pathless forests. Jumping from branch to branch. Of eons of time. In circular commotion. Of our gestures and our motions. Whether we forge our locomotion biologically. Or mechanically. Blasting ourselves sonically through space. Through international date zones. Through Europe overnight to Africa. In a fortnight. Around the world. We've not advanced our own creation. Through the space we've conquered. Only finding to our chagrin. Of hopping states and nations hemispheres and oceans. We have not bested time. But found it only relative. To what we could call progress. If we continued to delude ourselves awhile.

Our history is still. No different in the quality of the human. What we would define and call the human or the civilized. The intellectual. The rational. One of habit. Of delusion of acceptance of belief. Of tradition. But when it comes to any or to all of these. A concept is a concept. As easily reproduced. In man. Or chimpanzee. And like the chimpanzee. We collectivize against whatever threatens us. And fight to survive in our jungle. And chatter deafeningly. Through the murk. Through the vegetal life of the forest. Haunting us and biding its time. To weed over all we've hacked away. To build. To wrest. To spoil from another. For ourselves. In our feverish conquest. Marking the new industrial then the technological age. Hoarding what we've exploited. Hiding our hoards from the evolution of a conscience we say we're proud of. That which distinguishes civilization of homo sapiens. We say to our students of the liberal arts. From the orang-outang. Or the Dinosaurs. Who despite their small brains. Lived long. If we weigh their brains. Not their bodies.

Everything after all is relative. Rome as Empire and Republic. Lived to forge its forms along the Mediterranean. And the rivers to the Danube and the Elbe. And along the sands of Egypt. Almost to Parthia. Pushed back wind dust sand forest ice snow swamp jungle mountain river plain sea canal. Fought won lost battles wars legions territories states. Centralized decentralized nationalized and divided. Formed treaties and broke them along with *comitiatūs* and *triumviratūs*. Created families and parties and classes. United and destroyed them. Freed slaves. And sold men into slavery. Denounced and banished by its *lex Julia de pudicitia et de coercendis adulteriis* its sons and daughters and wives and husbands and brothers and sisters and nieces and nephews and aunts and uncles and mothers and fathers and sons and daughters by adoption and all the host of in-laws and friends and relatives and above all. The old Aristocracy of the old Republic. Finally drawn and quartered. Exhausted by taxes and centuries of breeding for public service. The knights the senators. The people of the Republic. The Empire. Came to respect and to believe in. In times of famine. Of wars which bled them at home. While the legions were fed and maintained in Asia. In Africa. And Rome's multiple elsewheres. While Rome dreamed to colonize the world. To Romanize it. To civilize it. To wrest itself and the territories. From receding back into the jungle and the swamp. And war and plunder. To stamp its soul. Its ego energy of man woman family morality public service and empire patriotism born of the long birth and struggle of the Republic. Into the genius and spirit and form and matter. Of the destiny. Of the symbol of itself. Which Rome did. And was to come to believe in. And which all that was European and Western. Was also Roman. Was also civilized. By virtue of the laws of its history. Of its tradition. By virtue of the forms by which its tradition was formed. The bridges the aqueducts the colisseums the amphitheatres the temples the fortresses the circuses the parade grounds the public baths the theatres the forums the walls of Hadrian the triumphal arches of Trajan the roman vias and fosse works and the villas the palaces and pillars and all the other monuments public and private. In partial and full decay. But there. As where they are. To say. We came. We saw. We conquered. For a longer moment than most. Longer by far than Alexander the Great. The one whose policy and dream we emulated most.

Are we then. Humanitas. Homo not so sapiens. *Nel mezzo del cammin.* Or about where history and ruins. Records where all of it began. The Age of Rome again. Of Romulus destroying Remus. Over and

over the same. In arid repetition. Wearisome and full of
vanitas. Except today we try to best our heritage of
human destiny. By greater possibility more total. Of the
end that will remind us of beginning. By not one empire
on the way to conquer the savage for his own good. But
many and at least 4. And the drama will be theatre for
the world. Which is both audience and performer. Conqueror and conquered. In the end. As in its own beginning. So Rome was. So probably we'll all be. Slavicized
by the Russians. Asiaticized by the Chinese and/or the
Japanese. Americanized by the Americans. Ostracized
and liquidized. By too much repetition. Of the law of the
jungle. The survival of the strongest. Not the best.
Which is hardly a survival. If it is at all. For what delusion of the rational ideal of being human. We if ever
for some short spasm of selfless surge heroically. To
biologically sport in accidental evolution of desperate
necessitous causation. In some wild dedicated self-
slaughter. As we clenched our fists in prayer. And not
destruction. Heavy-lidded. Sweating our fear and se-
men. In an orgy of joy and despair. Blinded by the dark
of our jungled self-victimization. In blackness and confusion. Hovering and afraid. As we burned in the fire.
And knew that we burned. And distinguished its light.
From the surrounding jungle of the long and familiar
night. And were curious and unafraid.

NINETEEN

THE ALL RICH VULNERABLE. That body of the soul. Of spirit. As conditioning for breath and breathing. Circumspect in shadowy protections of itself. Which. Wary in its cover and disguise. Metempsychoses. As oftentimes. And places as is deemed. For necessity's survival. Of what's pure.

Today the question is.
What is indeed the aspect of our lives.
That we can register. As full to breathing. Acknowledgement of all our sins. The one true structured part of self. Which worries not to reconvert itself. Much less another. Because existence in the essence of the being that it is. Prevents evasion and disquise. And squelching of the flames. The full regorgement. Driving in the passions of the chest and heart. Reiterating all that self-analysis would drive away.

So thus we abstract and disguise.

By way of cover. We would not be hurt.

Trampled by the hunters in the chase. To finally corner and expose and kill their prey. Because it's all a game you see. And sporting if you play. And if you don't. Well then who cares except the hunters. Who are supernumerary.

So thus with life itself. The life of man with man. With men. The species that must energize to kill. To stay alive. Upon the wheel of chance. Of accident. The roulette. With its sudden irreversible of tragedies. As wearying to our last breath desperation. And asseveration. That the persecutors persecute salvation-bearers. Perhaps it is that man upon this planet. Hardly really dares to face the issue in the question. Does or doesn't he. In utter full sincerity. Before the grim reality of its alternate. Does or doesn't he wish to be. The puppet surrogate scapegoat. Of salvation or annihilation.

There we have it now.

A grim embarrassment for most. We all like passionate despairing Homeric heroes. Such as swift-footed Achilles. Are bent on victory. No matter what the cost. For man. Despite his pious protestations to the contrary. Would rather play the act of thunderous

annihilation. Like a scourge or plague of sorts. Or fiery
stampede and rout. Than bask in quietudes of limpid
summer. With the green stalk. And the perfumed
flower. And the busy honey-making bees. With clouds
that overhang their cirrocumulus bellies of white un-
dulous vapor. Like a woman's drapery in voluminous
folds. Suspending over earth. To disgorge in down-
pours of abundance of the rains. All these and more.
With all the sky of purple dawns and copper sunsets of
our open plains and cacti cottonwood mesquite washes
of the West. And ferrous red earth and adobe clay
rancheritas and haciendas. And slum-like crumbling
walls of village after village. Of ruins that were ruined
by the Indian in his sieges. Or abandoned by the quick-
rich make-it-while-you-can gold miner. Who plastered
with old newspapers. The walls the wooden slats between the mud adobe. Where the cracks were. Where
the snow and cold came in. In the shivering grim
winters. Between good stakes and strikes. Where brawling in saloons. And gambling and drunkenness. And a
killing or two. Expelled the tension and the energy and
monotony. Of days that passed in fever of delusions. Of
hoping that the wheel would turn to you and no one
else. So that the chosen few and all its laws and superstitions of commitment. Would ring for you. And you
could enter heaven with your bag of ore. The loot. The
pickings. From the strike and diggings. Where cheating
in the blind thrust forward. And even grimmer despera-

tion of do or die. Became your thing. No matter what the cost to friend or foe.

So as in any struggle. Through the ages centuries millennia and eons of time. Man's time upon the planet he has chosen to biologize. And as he claims. To civilize. It's never very different. Between the now of our days of great technology. Efficiency in machines that serve for us to serve. Exactly what we serve. We don't for sure quite know. In our status creature comforts. That shield our delicate retrieval system of correct behaviour patterns. The question of the ages still assails us. As we try. The few who care. Who are not frightened by the very process of suggestion of its ultimate idea. *What then* is *good* or *bad* or *friend* or *foe*?

In relativity. We hide from answers. To any absolutes we morally would impose. Romanticizing what we would protect. The comfort and seclusion and the power we have fought and struggled for. To rise above the morass man eternally creates. Because he is a garbage of proliferating stench. And grim destruction of the beautiful. For all that's ugly in the trinket world of vanity he calls necessity. Where as it's all possession. Of all that others want as well. So because the other wants it. This gives as good a reason for the grab. Even if he shafts the other pulling on the same. The object is the thing you see. And not the principle. Of why the need for grab.

Which is why in our politicizing.

It's all so easy to manipulate. Not only things. But beings. Souls and spirits and idealisms and cultures and civilizations and traditions and faiths and beliefs. And the whole structured phenomenon of homo sapiens in a state of evolution. But which direction he could possibly evolve. Is just another grim guffaw of besting the grotesque of destiny.

For what is destiny or evolution. If not the history of man's manipulations. On the kingdom of mankind.

Mine is the kingdom. And the glory.

Oh no. Say that again. And I'll squelch your thrust and braggadocio. Like flatting an ant or swatting a fly.

The joke's on you Christ. As it was on Socrates.

It's all a game.

A commerce of coercion and manipulation. Whether it's playing bingo or its Las Vegas equivalent. For a church parish drive. Or shelling out to this or that charity. Boy Scouts. Or buying that sour mash of cardboard cookie. For the Girl Scout drive. Or the United or Red Cross Fund. Or the P T A game you are playing. Or any other game of Save The Children Fund. Or Salvation Army. Or Synanon. It all amounts to commerce of a kind.

By that I mean. The giving largely is some dark delusion. By which we stroke our comfortable behinds. Like cats that purr and lick their fur. Mysterious and alone. But more confused by sites we've set ourselves. Or others that have set them for us. So we believe what's good for us to believe in. Which others say is so. And so like Pavlov's dog. Conditioned to the bell which allays hunger. We salute the flag. Send our young boys now men. In the knowledge they've killed. Because they're told. To outlying jungles and sheds and swamps and rice fields. On headhunter borders. And in process of burning out the roots of trees that make the forests that hide the enemy. They swallow dust and with the help of a heroin addiction. They fight the fear and the grim guffaw of the nightmare of the devil that whispers through the crash of the upper of the shots and pills. And tells them its all a lie a delusion a travesty. What they're dying for. And the foulness of it all.

So even hunger. Is another of our manipulations of conditioning. The Irish child with rifle on the barricades of Belfast. Shooting taunting.

A Protestant children's rhyme:

Sleuter, slaughter, holy water
Harry the papishes every one
Drive them under and bate them asunder
The Protestant boys will carry the drum.

A Catholic children's rhyme:

On Saint Patrick's day, jolly and gay
We'll kick every Protestant out of the way
And if that won't do we'll cut them in two
And then send them to hell with their red, white and blue.

Urged on by the passions and paranoia of his elders. Sending their own to die as martyrs. Using life. The life of another. Of one's offspring as a commodity of tactic. So our guile is. The playing on erosion of our sensibilities. Hunger is patriotism. Patriotism. Hunger's satisfaction. Consuming the consumed. So all of us. As well as few. Told in one way or another. What to live for. What to die for. No matter what the price. For truth is relative Socrates. Despite your efforts about the virtue of the godliness within you. Of your god. It never was any different. Even if you tried. As valiantly indeed. The way you did. And died because you felt contingency with that which represents Athenian in spirit. The spirit of togetherness ah yes. Even you avoided banishment and isolation. And in his darkest moments. Glorious or vile. Man always fears and always has felt. The stigma of the ostracism of being alone. Of not wanting to be. Brother to Dragons. And companion to Owls. As Job cried out in anguish. Any and all of us can understand.

TWENTY

THE LONG SLOW LOPE of time. That foisted. And that fostered Caesars everywhere on Rome. Twin branched. And father-son. Augustus and Tiberius. On down to Vespasian and Titus and his brother Domitian. The augments. In the portents of their kind. To prove indubitably. How rule of man. Becomes the father in us all. To wish to find respect. And fervor of belief. Whatever kind. Of politics. Of gods. Of both. A Moses. Or an Abraham. Or Christ. The Father Son and Holy Ghost of Christianity. Or Julio-Claudio. Antonine. Whatever house or star. Conditions of belief. Are always of the same or comparable in kind. The blood of roots and family line. The tree and branch and species. All together now. As heretofore. Desired and pleasured for the asking. As man in child. And child in man we are today. A moment's dalliance in our all consuming principle of private utterance and pursuit. As onward plunging to obedience we would deny. Whereas the full reality of blows we give ourselves. To chastize. In the discipline of defeat. Reality so called. As masters of the G N P we were and sloth-like. In our sliding grasp. We yawn away our fears of being superseded. Like the ancient father sun king. Who'll be murdered by his son. A Laius. Superseded by an Oedipus. Who dreams bad dreams of fate. To mask his own ambitions. And does not wish to know what he does know. Inexorably to destroy. To muffle and disguise his sacrilegious and incestuous thrust. Self-blinded in the fears of retribution. Because we must succumb to all society's taboos of fears and boasts. Besides our own. Indubitably irrevocably. As linked by constellations of the mind's slow rationale. Of prejudice and belief. As fixed in human fate. As every zodiacal eternal coursing of the Bear. Orion. Betelgeuse. The Southern Cross. The Pleiades. Andromeda or Perseus.

So thus. The patterns of behaviour. And belief. As linked we are to one another. And to time. And change. And histories and dynasties. And weary violence. And all our neighings and denials. The passions of our thrust and challenge and rebuttals. Like the bucking of the stallion who will boot you. But who fears you finally. And succumbs. But never trusts his rider. And vice versa. Since the power will go up and down. And seesaw. One to other. Depending on who's riding. Or being ridden.

As thus comparison. So made. Between. Among the elements of change. The flux is just another metamorphosis of novelty. Disguising in a bafflement of gross surprise. What initially was there. But never seen.

The elements of politics. As natural to nations. As to blood and kin in families. The propaganda of each power complex. A ritual of behaviour's thrust upon the mind. As ancient and as modern as today. The discipline of faith and prejudice. Of hate and love and finally of confusion. Jumbled like a jigsaw on the consciousness. Enforcing its enforcement. In the action of the power grab. Which the populace. Like ants defend. And burdened by collective action. Build and fill the nest. The nation empire. Until it is knocked down.

So what is change for man.
Like art itself. It never will define a progress in the ultimate of final ends and causes. But simply exercise appeal in change. A movement in belief and form. Depending on the power of its thrust. Expensive or gratuitous.

But blood will spill in large and small. No matter how. And those of us. Or even our brothers. Insisting better to be red than dead. May therefore have a point in time. But perhaps not in destiny.

For destiny should be something that partakes. But most often doesn't. Of a heroism. Which we form in action. And like the artist of the language of the word or color or stone or sound or movement. Like any art worth half its substance. The form and thought are one. No artist ever practiced in a form. Without exerting action.

So with any action of the spirit. Action in the form is never passive. Otherwise it is no action.

To say no to sacrifice. I will not risk a dying. Is about the same as not risking living.

In destiny where we ourselves acknowledge having played. We live our moment actively upon the stage. And fight the opposition through the plot. The fate or destiny that rather would be blind. To these our sorrows and our joys and passions and desires. Unless we call an end to theatre. And insist the play is over fully and forever. We would be as Sisyphus. Eternally to renew our thrust. To do our thing. To roll the rock. The burden of our acceptance of the choice. Against the gravity that always pulls it down. After we have succeeded to defy defeat. Reaching the top. Only to momentarily get that glimpse of destination. As the rock falls down again. And we begin all over.

To surrender then in any form. Is to relinquish our position in a drama.

To become again as deadwood. In the full nonentity of being but the one who views the view. And not the one who makes it for you to view.

This is what it means to pacify the self. And not to care. This is what it means to not make a scene. But to be swept up in it. Like a vortex. To be swallowed in the tornado's eye. Is to succumb to fate or destiny. Not of your own making. Certainly *no way*. But of that other. Which becomes your own. Without your will to exercise a choice. Since choice means some kind of appropriation. Of a mark or symbol of possession. And this you haven't done. So the form is unresolved. As the action. Which is doing. Never was.

As thus to formulate. Societies where drugs have taken hold. The mescaline the acid the grass the uppers and the mixers and the downers. Of every thrust and kind. Immobilizes in a blue funk or joy beyond belief. The phantasmagoria of worlds of never been. That suddenly seem to be. As you play in a deadly game not of a world which is. But which excites taboo and totem. The nonentity of passive non-resistance playing god and the devil. Destroying and creating nothing. In the end. Because there is always an end. Just as there is a means. To anywhere. And somewhere. As well as to nowhere. Just as there is always a choice. To destiny. To fate. If you wish to choose.

TWENTY-ONE

AT LAST. AS THE CHANCE for wear. Upon the shadows of the days as hours. To wander. Wondering if this is so. That being of the consciousness. As is. To flow beneath the suppuration. And to purge as blood. The very essence of the fever. The all or nothing of one's very consciousness. To feel and foil as man. As losing. Or as winning. On about or there. What voodoo in its sad full measure of the hate. That seethes and roils us. We Americans. Which hardly out of bush. That frontier of the romance of the dust and sagebrush. And the grim coyote howls. And slithering rattler with his sudden strike. Where stones are overturned or violated. In the golden mellow burn of sun rays of the Southwest desert. The cholla barrel prickly pear and other cacti. Their hidden reservoirs of fruit and water. For the birds to feed on. And the gaunt and ghostly giant fingered green saguaro. Where the nests are. Where the songs of territorial occupation trill upon the echos of the lonesome rocks. The buttes the mesas. In their faults and lacoliths and batholiths and anticlines. Where silence of the centuries erodes upon the recent stalking of apaches and of sioux and ute. Upon that cliff that now embraces you in shadow. Nothing more. The blood bath of the swarm of gnats. As crushed beneath between the spokes of wagon wheels. Encircling for protection. In a moment lost in time. Shaking fingers and clenched fists. As poised in fear as much as anger and frustration of the death to come. Where life refused to die. And fought for territory and for just the space for soul and purpose of itself. To saunter. Lies down in darkness. In the blood of carnage. Spilled against the line of purple in horizon. On the ribboning of the sunset's haze in dust. After the parry and the thrust. The whoops. The war cries. And the scalpings. And abductions of the women who will breed no more the white man's paleface. But will spread for germination of another seed to breed. And belly forth like horses or like sows. A new breed half-breed born of conquest and of rape. And hate and lust and blood and passion and surrender to both enemy and sex. As opposites must do. Eventually. Reunion of the flesh. As earth to thrusts of seasons and to storms. Where violence is succeeded and preempted. By the feed of hunger and of need. As much as destiny requires. To affirm. And reinforce the breed.

And so no stones of mountains that jut forth their thrust upon the desert plains. Is without its history of passionate here and now as well as then. Which made the here and now. True. There are no Rosetta Stones to prove it. What Americans call history. The carnage of erosion of the red man's seed. Which had proliferated on the prairies of the West. As well as North and South and East. Like constellations of the heavens. In their large and shining leisure of the nomad. A gypsy life of hunting. Based on seasons of the belly's need. Of men and tribes. Of wives and children. Of counting sunsets. Like the course of zodiacal time by stars at night. And worship of the great heat magic of the sun by day. And life was simple. There was only a question of the enemy to be feared. And as he was so often. More as not familiar. Another red man of another clan or tribe. To scalp to vanquish and sometimes to admire or despise. The danger was familiar. And destiny was not a stranger. Until the stranger came. In waves of wagon trains. With death that came from powder of the barrel of a gun. In cattle drives that dusted all the footpaths and the secret byways. Which knew nothing heretofore but hardened weary cactused calloused stalking. Of the indian who found the waterfalls and bottomless springs both steaming in their vesicules of heat. As well as icy in their floes of snow melt. Always for his people. As a gift. A duty. A thanksgiving. And a burden. All a part of life as lived. In steady sameness. As the colors of the hues of rainbows after rain. Until the time span. And the life span. And destiny and death were altered. And even birth would never be the same. The hunger and starvation. No longer accidents of nature. But of fate that based itself on hate. On man white against man red. On a thrust of struggle. To wrest the earth. The bounty. The solitude and mystery of seasons and of cycles. And turn them quite around and upside down. And fence in wildness in the capturing of animals. And the rape of earth. As much and more for profit. As for grim necessity. To climb the ladder of the species man. By starving those upon what we considered of the lower rung. By running down the lordly food supply and pelf of wealth and warmth and paternalistic splendor of his bounty of the earth he thundered over. As all the plains were his. And the red man berthed and flourished and worshipped and wore his splendor and totemed himself after the skins the fur the bones as amulets. Of the mighty bison-buffalo. Slaughtered in ravines. That wiped him out as well as those he nourished and he magicked.

So blessings on you. Wild Bill Hickok. Calamity Jane. Kit Carson. Coronado and Cortez. And Buffalo Bill. The friend of kings and presidents. Pony Express Rider, Buffalo Hunter, Frontiersman, Army Chief of Scouts. America's and the world's greatest huckster. Barnum of the West. And your Wild West Show. Guns saddles trophies silver buckles safaris dude ranches stock frauds. Neronian circuses of Africans Moors Dancing Girls Elephants Pythons Half-breed Indians Mexican Sharp Shooters Annie Oakley. Gal Equestrians Western Cavalry Cowboys and Cow-punchers. And the whole darn breed of America's bummy seedy dustgrit greedy seething whiskey-bellied cowpoke huckstering lily-livered puritan hell-fired purgatoried god-fearing bible-toting man-hating indian-killered bushwacker mine and cattle stealer desperado, hired-gun vigilante justice rough and ready roistering bite the dust, hangman railroad gangman and the whole glamor bag of smart-aleck frontier get-with-it success or succumb philosophy of exploit or be exploited. And carry the white man's burden. Which happens to be a bag of gold. And not his sins be hanged. Be hanged if you do. And be hanged if you don't.

TWENTY-TWO

I READ TODAY ABOUT SOME languages dead and gone. Extinct. Defunct. Whatever word. The insult is the same. I mean to life and living. As the case might be. Or even was. Or might have been. It is a strike we never can recover from. That universal darkness over all. When language dies. The breath of spirit. In the act of grim survival. Whether love or hate desire greed gregariousness pride lust covetousness or what the human improvisation of the play. Charade will call the players. As the prompter. In the prompting box the lines. The movement and the urge is but the same. For peoples as for players as for playwrights. To sing some tune of life and destinied survival. However grim or sad or glad or silly-foolish simple as it seems. Or complex in a way and time that brooks no interference from its smashing success. Like crushing out a fly. The god you play. As imbecilic and as sotted stupid. As the tool you flourish. Whoever plays the god to squash the

fly. Uses nothing but a thing of mesh and wire plastic. Plastic's the thing in fly swatters nowadays. Plastic for cleanliness and efficiency. It lasts and lasts and lasts. And the flies. They just come and come and come. But we'll beat them in the end. Or so we think. Before they mutate into just another kind of bug. And bug our future generations of plastic kings and salesmen. Where flies as well as people will succumb to being swatted. And efficiency will reign on life and death. And death will be as clean and clear and logical and acceptable and smilingly inevitable and all embracing. As life is today. And struggle will end. And heaven will be here and now what it's always been. But only dreamed. Except it will be real. And life will die. And death will live. Ah pardon. John Donne. You were wrong you see.

To return now to our original surprise.
The notice of history in recording dead languages. Why bother? A lesson in geography perhaps. Well reason enough. You draw your own conclusions reader. Think of it as a game. Your language is alive as you are. The game's just part of showing off some scholarship you and I picked up in a desk encyclopedia—the *Columbia-Viking* to be exact.

We'll set our limitations to this hemisphere. *The play's the thing/Wherein we'll catch/The con-*

science of the king. It's never different regardless of who
plays the king. It's always them not us. There but for the
grace of ?God? Go I? Are you kidding? Drama's no
game, no entertainment buddy-sister-friend. It's life.

Let's raise the curtain then to our over-
ture. The leitmotif. Of this today's our theme. Related to
the one of yesterday or yesteryear. Here goes: These
then are dead languages. So designated by an asterisk in
the list. But we'll just list the dead. And not the living.
And thus no asterisk will have to clarify our brains.

> *Yana—North East California*
> *Esselen—South of San Francisco*
> *Salinan—San Luis Obispo Coast*
> *Chumashan—Santa Barbara coast*
> *Tonkawa—Austin region, Texas*
> *Karankawa—Middle Texas coast*
> *Atacapa—SW La., SE Texas*
> *Umpqua—Northwestern, et al., Athapascan*
> *Pecos—Towa from Tanoan*
> *Pojoaque—From Tewa branch of Tanoan*
> *Miami, Illinois, Powhatan, Natick, Narragansett,*
>   *Mohegan, Pequot, from Algonquian, all extinct.*
> *Ofo, Biloxi, Tutelo—Ohio group from the Siouan*
> *Missouri from Mississippi of Siouan as likewise*
>   *Kansa from Dhegiha of stock Siouan.*

Which shows you does it not. How Americans. The first fruits of a continent of plenty. In a paradise of nature. Died unnaturally. Invaded by forked-tonguers. Great with God. So Adam named the many species to serve man. So Genesis insists he did. So man served man. Enslaved or butchered by his kin. So civilization savaged. And cultures multiplied. And disease and death and extinction. With all the blood and carnage of our laboratory earth. Bringing death to the Stone Age. As Adam brought death to his kind. So we Adams bring death to our kind. First we kill them. Our enemy. And then their culture. And with the culture. So the communicant. The microbe breeding life and continuity. That defies extermination. Until finally no culture remains to feed upon. And the language the placenta loses nourishment. And no further breeds. As breath of life recedes. So does the word. Logos-Soul. Spirit-Flesh-Word. All forspent.

Oh yes. The tribal Stone Age. Like a ghost. So ghastly to our spirit of technologized man. Remains in shreds and fragments here and there. The Tasadays of the Philippines. Sons of Adam wearing T-strings of orchid leaves and bark. Against the witches. So they say. Believing in the devil. Their food: the pith of palms and tubers of the wild. Their traps of bamboo spears. And roasted monkey is their Stone Age delicacy barbecued. And the leaf is their umbrella from the rain.

Paradise for the Tasaday. And their brother. The Sanduka. The Xeta of Brazil. And the Akuriyo. The Parakana and the Asurini of Brazil. And the other sons of Adam. Of Stone Age Man. Wherever in South America or New Guinea. Or why not Asia. All prove that Genesis is right. And none of them are christians are they. They're just people who live in Paradise. Who've been discovered. Sooner or later. Like the Indian-American. Who must die once he is corrupted. And corruption simply means discovery. And discovery brings enlightenment and civilization and disease and more corruption. And the evil of experience. And the devil is ourselves. No longer some bad dream of spirit or of voodoo that we try to exorcize. Only in Paradise is Satan a Snake. In civilization he is ourselves.

This is the story of why Adam dies and Stone Age Man dies and why we destroy our discoveries of innocence by experience.

TWENTY-THREE

Light over sky   if princes lie
what hath man to steer thereby?
An hundred lords respect themselves? Not even!
By that the less revere each other, or heaven.

THE CONFUCIAN ODES
Ezra Pound

ONWARD A LITTLE MORE with the march of the tongues of the cult. The cultures and breed banks of biologic man. Sociologized by fate. Of other's choosing. And of seizing. Not his own.

Of Language. And its rise and fall.

Of Poetry. And Myth. And Dream.

And Reason in its true awakening. Of Truth. Socratic for a moment. Dialectical. Where conversation sang. And berthed and bathed. The steady gaze and hue of light. That far and wide. Refused to flinch at substance of itself. Did not digress or shrink in shadow of retreat. Which never feared exposure. For like sunlight. Grew joyous in the warmth and blaze. Reflection and refraction. Which multiplied in fruition. Of the harvest which it cultivated staunchly. Without fear of ghosts or witches or of thunderbolts from up above. Or fires from below. The truth was like a voyage of discovery. Man made and man pursued. And no god of fear or awe or anger or ambition. Could dare dare the challenge. The thrust beyond the limitations of all taboo. Man the totem of the strange the human in himself. Beyond beyonds. Sailing. Seething in the waters of abyss. Where Scylla and Charybdis. Were not some outer reefs of raw fear challenge. But just the tissue fabrications of the flesh curled. Poised to strike itself down. As a part and particle umbilical. Which the first sung heroes of death's defiant struggle. Where the Logos of the Word as Truth as Song as Pictures Dreams and Joyous Celebrations of the Life to Come. Announced themselves in full Imagination. And burned the shadows of darkness. With its Rays. The New Religion came. And thus it conquered ritual and destiny. And the gods did not rejoice from heaven or Olympus. Man reigned in his own heaven. And earth heaved in the sin of the insult it received. As the garden of the gods overturned. And out came Man. No longer cultivator and a child of joy. But exploiter and creator and destroyer. Of himself and kind.

The bacteria. The culture and gestation. The fissions and divisions. The seed as sown in every breeze of time. The seasons of breeding and of overturning. As all land bridged and groaned beneath the weight and push and thrust of migratory man. Who spread and dug and ditched and canaled and colonied like ants. And found. what was good and evil in himself and others. And named all that he found and made in himself and others. And found he could covet more than he needed. And survival and destruction became a game. No longer seen thru the flicker of reflection of the fire. On the wall of the cave. He was no longer cave man. He could dream and scheme and linguify and multiply. Liquidating in his path. All that didn't yield.

The tongue of man forks. And speaks in many tongues. Dividing the world into realms and kingdoms and principalities and sovereignties of hell and heaven light and darkness. Zoroastrian Mithraian Christian Confucian Brahmian Druidian Babylonian Nibelungian Jovian or Jahvehian. All in the name of cults and sects and tongues and cultures and civilizations.

            These then. Of Deaths. And Entrances. The shadow and the substance. The myth of fairy. And the tale of truth. Of Politics. And politeness. Of nudity and disguise. The eye. All seeing. As the eye. All masquing. Of change and repetition. Of death and resurrection. The tales are told and played in tongues and fabrications. And imagination is the curtain that must fall. To separate the rulers from the ruled. To hide the truth behind the scenes. While entertainment and deception play their part. In every theatre of the world that's ever been. The source and fount. Of what we call society. Its history and times. In the language of the tongue. That sang and trilled and filled the heavens with its elevation. And that fell. Encaged. Imprisoned. After it manured the ground. And cultivated harvests of its own inbreeding. And disease and infestation wracked and wrecked it to the core. Sterilized and neutralized and exhausted to extinction. After seasons and centuries and cycles of its own deception. Treasoned from within. By the cancer of the fruit that withered. Because it was refused its Truth. Which Man discovered in his distant time of Sin and sad Experience. As berthed from Innocence. That never will be Innocence again. That Garden of Paradise. Being but the dream. The exploration through the tongues and peoples of mankind. With all his miffed attempts to spread his wings. Like Icarus. Or defy the Sun. Like Phaeton. Chained like Prometheus. His defiance. Hacked and eaten. Like his liver. Circumscribes him. Like the destiny he defies. His Rock of Ages. To which he is eternally enchained.

Onward and upward and downward. The tongues of the *Book of the Dead*. As the Word. The Logos. Ceased. Like outworn garments. One by one. Discarded. In death. They tell their tale of dissolution. Unused and useless. Led out to pasture. Gone to seed. In the garden of time. Exhausted and defeated. Extinguished. By the light of culture. Of civilization. Of deception. Or of truth. That finally irrevocably failed. The language that you speak today. However true or false. Tomorrow too will surely die as these have proven theirs have done. Only the letters. The syllables of their trial and trust and thrust. The records of their human gesture. Momentary as this may seem. And just as vain. May just remain.

This tale and tablet of the dead. Like the unknown soldier. In now and future wars. Is as irrevocable and irreversible. As it is repetitious and incomplete. But here it is:

Franconian-Old and Middle

Old Saxon
Lower Franconian
Old English, Middle English-Middle Scots
Old Norse
Old Swedish
Gothic, of Germanic as the family
Gaulish
Middle Welsh, Cornish
Goidelic-Old, Middle
Umbrian
Old, Classic, Medieval Latin
Vulgar Latin, Old Italian, Old French
Dalmatian
Oscan, of Italic and Celtic as their families
Ionian, Homeric Greek-Classical Attic Hel-
*   lenistic Greek, Koine, Biblical Greek (OT,*
*   NT), Byzantine Greek*
Doric, Choral Doric, Corinthian-Aolic-
*   Cyprian-of the family Hellenic or Greek*
Slavonic (Old Church), of the Slavic or Slavonic
Old Prussian of the Baltic, as its family
Avestan, Old Persian-Pahlavi, Sogdian
Vedic, Sanskrit
Prakrit (several languages), Pali of Indo-Iranian
*   as their families*
Tokharian A (of Turfan), Tokharian B
*   (Kuchean)*
Classical Armenian-of Tokharian and Armenian
*   respectively*

Hittite (Kanesian), Hieroglyphic Hittite, Luwian, Lycian, Lydian—of the family Anatolian
Babylonian, Assyrian, Nuzi Akkadian, of Akkadian as family
Old Canaanite, Moabite, Phoenician, Punic, Hebrew, Ugaritic—of Canaanite as family
West Aramaic: Biblical, Palestinian, Modern Syriac, Mandean, of Aramaic as family
Andalusian Arabic, Himyaritic—of Arabic as family
Geez—of Ethiopic as family
Egyptian, Coptic—of Hamito-Semitic as family
Old Libyan, Guanche (Canaries)—of Hamitic as family
Standard Written Chinese, Ancient—of Chinese as family

TWENTY-FOUR

WHICH AS URGE. FOR by another feature of the self. That searching in your own American of days. The hours of the years. The centuries try. To reconfigure. What it's all about. To be as other than the featureless in crowds. That glide by systems of their own full making. Of the family person idiot or friend. The stranger in us all. Collective and together now. We flail and groan. And wonder. From the corners of our eyes. If we can be as trusted as the ones we dare to trust. And like the children of another day and time. That not far distant from ourselves. Gave vent to these our searchings. And our blind confused imaginings. Where grant for place and style. In the features and configurations of the world we've made. The one that we've inherited. Despite our sentimental looking backward of the child. Sucked back. Like lollipops and sugar pills and candy cotton. All that features of our prior landscape. Ballooned us in our all-consuming careening funny house and wonder-wheels of pleasure. As we froze with wonder and with laughter in regurgitating mad intoxication. Belly laughing in our pain of too much excess of the dreams of fantasies gone wild. The scenic-railway of our goose-pimply fright. Of heights and downdrafts. In the updraft dizziness of make-believe. The Luna Parks in Coney Islands. Of our dreams. Canarsie. Disneyland. The all too wholesome unwholesome. Togetherness of our dreams. The jelly apples sticking all its cinnamon and sugar to our ribs. The rooms of mirrors. And the stage-door Indian. The cowboy with his pistol at his side. The freaks of human zoos of pleasure. Which always hid the pain of stare and glare. The bearded ladies. And the Siamese twins. The female-breasted male. The pygmy families with pointed encephalitic mongoloided craniums. The man with the fish-scaled body. Or the monkey tail. The hucksters shouting instant magic herbals. While the Indian. Not so wooden. In his cigar store garb. Yawned and braced his bony age-lined fingers. For the grasp of grab. Of whatever greenbacks you could spare. To bet your bottom dollar. On the heap good white man's medicine. That would cure his pain. The ulcer that was "guaranteed" to disappear. And hair that knew to grow exclusively on balding pates. And all the gimcracks of the penny arcade machines. The fortune-telling lady in her glassed-in cage. Where the iron crane would dip and furrow. And out popped Halloween candy and a popcorn souvenir. A paper or a tin or plastic toy of sorts. Or maybe gumballs and a fortune card that never lied. Because the fantasies. Leaped and jounced in flashing blinding images of neon. On and off. But provisional to what you yourself believed. The gullibility disguised by confectionaries and disguises. The noise and press of crowds. The gestured hoarse throats of the barkers. Positioned. Like Cerberus to scare. While grinning. You would take it in your stride. This River Styx of tawdry derelicts. Glittering in their tinfoil and confetti. Yawning their gap-toothed tobacco-stained smiles. Coughing against their ribs in the smoke-filled stage doors. Between shows. The knife throwers. The flame shooters. And their doll-moll accomplices. In fraud. The whole bag of circuses. Of dreams more painful in their horror of all that's cheap. Than all the wistful wide-eyed wonder. Of a child.

So. As adult fully so American. The dreams so paranoid go on. Enclosed within the sexless squaredom Main Street. Of Mickey Mousedom and plastic flowers and animals and waxworks and electronic machines and good old USA songs of patriotic hat-tossing heart-throbbing salutes and cheers. The apple pie fried chicken finger-lickin good of Motherhood and Country and good old Dad. And frat hugs and banging banjo tinkling pianos. And shuffling show-biz tap shoe black-face routines of pre-Civil War Mississippi boat side shows. Remind us of the fun we had. Playing the roles of worlds of make-believe. Which no kidding now. We let ourselves believe. Or why should we arabesque. With joy at the grotesque. Because it never was. Or better still. Always is. Because unlike a lot of other peoples. Of other cultures. Crawling across the flash bulb remembrances and shocks of history. The make-believe of all our antiseptic gadgetry. Is far more real to us. Than nature flesh man god sea wind mountain valley prairie sun moon stars continents peoples myths rituals traditions soul spirit mortality heaven hell immortality transubstantiation. The laying on of hands. Or benedictions or prayers or embraces like a Spanish abrazo or a French kiss.

To make. And not to be or feel. To perform like the erector-toys. And be efficient. As we unperfume the sweat and perspiration of our human cells. And choke and cloak them in invisibility and full neutrality. As sterile as death. Which latter is a story told. Not by time or the supernatural. But only by the embalmer. Even death's a craft. The illusion of life that was. No longer is. A machine of wax. Before which we pay our numbed and dumbed respects. No more no less in tribute and respect. Than what we owe to all our gadgetry of other worlds. Of these our times material. Where matter is not earth or sea or air or food or spirit or substance. But a symbol a doll a machine a means of barter of exchange. An annuity. A mortgage. Insurance.

Interest. Shares on the stock exchange. Real estate. Bonds. Social security. Pensions. The culmination of our dreams of not so long ago. When we turned away. Did not look back. Like Orpheus. Or Lot. But grimly. As a people. So we thought. United in our dreams. Rebellious to a past we wanted to forget. Succeeded better than we had ever dreamed. Bull-dozed. All the idylls of the Paradise we found here. Crushed myths and rituals and customs and beliefs. And languages of other men's dreams not our own. Destroyed the Stone Age remnants that we found. The lion of the plains. The bison. Tamed the Continent. Contained it. Like a time capsule we hoped would explode upon the world. And not ourselves. Goose-stepped with our panaceas for new life. Into the 20th century we had always dreamed about. A world where flesh and spirit would die in machines. Where machines and the artifice of disguise and imitation and substitution and alike but not the same. Of equivalences in equivocations. And similarities. And fraudulencies. Would be worshipped and preserved. Our civilization. A monstrous monolith. A grotesque of fantasy which never varies. In its Coney-Island. Of our mindless mind. That searches and suffers and wonders. What happened to those unfulfilling dreams.

TWENTY-FIVE

THE FIRST AMERICAN. WAS not of course the first American. Not so much. The difficulty of it all to place. In Time and History. As the grim conviction of it all. To recognize remembrance. In a vague nostalgia. Which we now. To clarify and color. By the romance. Of the suffering of past pain. By destiny. A certain kind of view of life. Of some collective of belief. Rejecting all the spiny growths that haunted and voodooed from the past. Which could be so easily and tacitly summarized. Was persecution of every form and kind. Which Europe was so expert in. Despite its bulbous onioned layered wealth of time and history and civilization. The cruelty was there. The bloodshed. And the sacrifice. The burnings and the persecutions. The tribal burdens of its tax collections. The grim privations of its many peopled cruelties. The hordes of hunger and the passion to survive. Which pressed upon the Roman-Germanic lines. The *limes* of the frontiers of the West.

The grim parade of alamanni suevi vandal hun. And all the mongol horde of populi barbaric. Always breaking in upon the feudal structure of oppression. To knock it down and build another of their own. The same the same. As how should Man. The homo sap -- be any different than the fool he is. Full of vast delusions from his beguiled befogged brain. That seethes in swamps in liquids of his own biology of water. How should matter of the spirit rise from water of his vegetable of brains. Buried as it is in water. As his name is writ in history and time. "Whose name was writ in water." At least 95%. To speak of biologically.

How puny funny. To point the finger at himself with pride. When drowning's almost all too good. For an earthbound piece of rotted grimy proto-plasmic lumpen glob. So easy in his lies and easier corruptions. Presumptuous to romanticize his cruel hates. In a religion of a sort. To fit the need of climate. Of historical extension. Of the spatial geographic destiny. That American as we are. And so declare. Manages to gild the package. In an emblem of nobility. That substitutes for the European one we've left behind. Deliberately. In a fit of pique. Then later. More sorrier than sad. We glorified all our cruelty of superior acquisitiveness. And Christianized its leaven of earthbound animal feral greed. And called it something of the spirit of the Cross. The White Man's Burden. So we sanctified it.

Burying our guilt with something of an old familiar calling and refrain. Sanctimoniously we turned the other
cheek. Not to others' cruelty but to ourselves. The
cruelty we perpetrated and forgot. In the orgy of our
righteousness we called the will and will of God. To
strike where and why? Why to civilize the continent
from end to end. From sea to sea. *God Bless America. My
country tis of thee. Of thee I sing.*

          I wonder then indeed which is more
savage.

          The will to civilize. Destroying in an
effort to create.

          Or the destiny to follow Nature as Nature
is. And accept the seasons and the tides of rivers. And
the phases of the moon. And the winds and currents of
the air. As vegetable and life. To growth and harvest. To
be thankful in a ritual. Organic to the sun and stars. As
well as man. To draw blood. To allay the hunger of the
tribe. As well as symbol of the brother kinship. Of the
one whose wrist you've slashed in blood friendship and
life loyalty.

          Yes. To be primitive as the Red Man. Was
not to be American. And so we could not let him be.
Barbarian to us. As we to him. But he was primitive.
And we because of history. We could not in the end

deny. Altho we tried in turning our backs upon the Continent. From which we came. To turn our shoulders on the wheel and grindstone. Upon the Continent to which we came. In the sacrificial thrust forward. Declared ourselves the children of our fathers. And acted just as they would have acted. Had they been us. Which indeed they were. They being that. From which we came. So we colonized.

And just what does it mean to colonize? To Europeanize-Americanize. The march of the *civispolis*. Onward and onward. West to East. To Hellenize. To Romanize. To Europeanize. To Nationalize. To Barbarize. Over and Over. To Americanize. Which meant to Europeanize. And colonize. And barbarize over again. The culture that we found. Only to hate it and destroy it.

We European-Americans. We were not to live like nomads. Like Jobs or Ishmaels upon this Continent. We would contain it like men. Like the Europeans we were. Before we were Americans. Destroying the genus of place. The community of Nature. For our own. Enclosuring ourselves. Like the grass we grew. For the cattle we fattened and sold. And stole from our neighbors. And branded theirs as our own. Because our land was the land of liberty. Which meant we were free. Until we were lynched or shot.

The only danger from without.
Was not the Indian. Routed corrupted and dismembered. By ourselves. But ourselves. Loyal as we were. Only to the law of accident of chance. To the victor belong the spoils. Catch as catch can. Damned if you do. And damned if you don't. That is obey or disobey. Bible tote and drink abstain. Whiskey carouse and devil arouse.

They're both American. Like Janus we're two-sided. Opposites of the self we're torn between. We love God. And really hate him for the Puritans he's made us. Corruption's not just around the corner. It's here to stay. Right where we live and breathe.

We judge our fellows. To be as miserable as ourselves. For man my fellow Americans. Says the present Father of our Country Presiding Officer of the Elect and Non-Elect. In Wasp America. Is a sinner. And we're all sinners we Americans. We might as well accept. And bow our heads. And sing our dirty anthems to the devil. Imagining in our own duplicity. That the deity we deify. Materializes and sanctifies our own materiality. That our ambitions our conquests of the Continent. Have been approved from on high. While the rivers sludge. And the oceans stagnate. And the air pollutes. And the kills of pests. Save the plant. And chemicalize our blood.

Cancering ourselves on efficiency. We outsmart nature in every manner or means. The age of artifice it is. A renaissance of the *Book of the Dead*. The zombie world of plastic and atomic missiles. Detergents phosphates. The huckstering religion of sell it. Shove it down their throats. The gag's on them. The suckers that live on sell them more and more and anything they'll buy. To fill a need declared by fiat of the combine cartel corporation of the brotherhood of Mammon and Beelzebub.

Too long we've lingered in the mountain winter snows and worshipped clouds of summer and felt the moisture with relief in bursts of rain and smelled the plankton and the seaweed of the oceans and the sweet and sour smell of new mown grass and hay and remembered the creamy curds of butter churned from milk. Or lobsters fat from lazy growth in cold and icy seas. Or bread with germs of wheat or rye or oats. That pricked your nostrils with their warm and yeasty smells. And cheese that festered germs in natural fermentation.

Goodbye goodbye to blue skies without haze and golden tangerine peach dawns and purple sunsets. As the chest chokes with sulphide and the eyes smart with monoxide fume and the tongue laps like a cat its fur the water of life commixed with ground garbage chemicaled and detergent and phosphate-cycled and recycled. As we lap in the poisons we adjust to and allergyze in.

Hail O *Coffee Rich*.
Contains no milk or milk fat.
Ingredients: Water (?), Corn Syrup Solids Vegetable Fat Sodium Caseinate Sodium Citrate Polysorbate 60 Sorbitan Monostearate, Mono-And-Diglycerides, Carrageenan, Artificial Color (Beta Caroteen).

Prosit. May you live long and your death be brief or should it be: May you die long and your life be brief.

Who or what is going to suffer for our sins? Or will the suffering be patience of the pain. Enduring to the very end of these our sins. Of commission and collusion and omission of the soul and spirit. The vegetable of matter as its given as it breathes. Destroyed from life the way it's always functioned into life. Until once more as probably of before. And many times. In eons of the geologic past. It berthed and slumbered and then berthed again. Despite the foreign interference of some body. Or a germ that would erupt. And blow the lid right off the top of such a superstructure. Such as man. By far the greatest threat. To both himself. The planet of his origins. And the chain of life. That brought him forth. Endangered. By its own creation.

TWENTY-SIX

WHERE THEN AS BE.
As how to try for.
The onrush hauntingly. Of quality. Of heat gone sour. As the trembling lips of female genitalia. So the upsurge passions of the hour. Which would be denied. As full forced and flavorful. To foam and milk the chase. The being of the sex proclaimed. Which tentacled to flesh as crawl. Befogs the vision of the smile as sin. The spectacles. As rims for thought. To frame the word. And focus on the passions in abstractions of the syllables of thought. Extruding blood of bile. The via pacifica of prejudice denied. For a priori is a sin of pride. No less of sex you see. And you must bend and bend and bend and bend. Until the back breaks. And the buttocks. And all the rest. To reaffirm. In womanly embrace. Between the thighs he holds you viced. The tubular as steel. No wasted flesh upon its cap. As smooth as stone. As jelly in the mash. You force upon. With every

vestige of the force. Athletically to bear. As bared upon the open wound of thirst. Where. As the parted lips do feed. Between the legs. And foam their fever. In the substance given as received. So sex remains and is. For what it is. Consummate in the sharing of the serve. The game of it is not a fight or contest of the mind. Contrary to the thought of what you'd think or possibly believe. As art is. Delicate to receive. The nourishment as full. As frozen to behold. Where fixed in form. It bears upon its axle. And its nuts and bolts and pigmentations. And the movement in the silence of itself. Received the way it shouts. Or tenderly caresses all of you. The mind and body. Blowing in a windless wind. So still that death and life are one. Stentorian. In the echoes of the self-feared pride. As bulbous to the onion. As the flower to the plant. As seed bursts pustules. And the gangrene spills. The poison. In the excess. Is a health of consummation. Ready for attack. To be attacked. Because where else would excess go. But to receive. Where weak the vessel would succumb as well as fight. As death-in-life and life-in-death. Hangs death or life. In balance of the one or other. So the solitude of lust. Beatitudes the mind. In flesh as feed. As fuel. As food. As hunger sated in the wash of thirst. Which formerly denied. Is then satisfied. As river fever. In its wake of tide. Subsiding after rhythm of the rage-blown fever. Fully as itself. The vast. As plethora. To sky and symbols. Crashing. As the stars. Dilating in the pupils of the eyes. The tension as it builds. And so again again again. The energy. As sport for what it is. Not unisexed. But doubly. As the share between. For two or more. Depending on the size and quality of appetite you share.

Where but to be.

As frozen into flight. The form you tremble by. As gender. Reiterates its seed of dream. Which reaffirms you solidly. To state your case. The woman or the man is not the question. The sex is there accepted. No need of teasing and beastifying what you know is there. As sex is. So is mind. No one more than other. So it seems. The dreams of Molly Blooms as notwithstanding. For repetition beyond the point of repetition. Is no longer repetition. Not even art. But repetition. Pure and simply for the tease. The obscene which no longer serves. Because the "Thing" of Molly Bloom. No matter how she twists and turns and groans and grunts and blushes. Is clothed in all the fetishes they lived by then. As stuffed with eiderdown and horsehair as the place of lay. And blush your sins away my dear my dear. You couldn't take it off then. No more than the disguise you wore. As undergarment to the bare behind. No more than names or dreams or gadgets nowadays. To flavor and to ravish. As a sauce on oysters. Which covers. To uncover all the flavor. Imprisoned in the flesh. Which my dear you know now. Don't you know. You fag. You gay. You lesb. You women's libbie. Or politico-militico. Bra and Jock burner.

Flag and Draft card. And all the other burners ravishers rapists. Of their dreams of liberation of the self. And self-destructs. Destroying all the neighers and deniers. The Houyhnhnms. So animally pure. The Prufrocks and the Street Folks. Who sing "murder and create." And just don't dream about it. But who do you know. No Molly Blooms who bloom their blushes in the dreams Victoria bouqueted. And Freud fumed and Joyce re-joyced. In titillations teasing. Like confetti. The porno of the boudoir. Not the street. The Mansons of the thrill kills. Are as real now. Without comparing them to im-age or identity. Libidinous as seems. Ideas of murder or create. As seems now is. As being. In the life of now. Of spirit thwarted. On a treadmill. In a funnyhouse. Where murder in the world is dying. And murder in the telly vibe tube of the news of global plug-in. As we tune McLuhan style. And wrap around ourselves. The en-velope of thrills as sado-masochist. As all the heap of celluloid and plastic visuals. Of news residuals elect-ronic in the void. That channels. Tunes you in. To several theatres of war around the globe. Just take your pick.

Belfast-Northern Ireland
Lebanon-Syria
Libya-Chad
Iran-Iraq
Russia-Afghanistan
Ethiopia-Eritrea-Somalia
Angola

Zimbabwe (Rhodesia)-Mozambique
Namibia (South-West Africa)-South Africa
Kampuchea (Cambodia)-Vietnam-Laos
Guatemala
Nicaragua
El Salvador

Israel and the PLO in Lebanon and the rest of the Middle East. The last about to resume. After a too-long intermission. Between cease-fires.

What difference is there then? To see or to perform. To push the button and relax upon the sofa. While the pus bursts. The blood streams. The limbs blow up. The shots from shells. From rifles cannons machine guns air missiles. Provide the theatre of the real. No fiction here. But hard to be believed. We shake our heads. And dully. With the eyes glued. And the ears attuned. To the sound and sight of news that's always bad. The TUBE discharges electronically. And so we're narcotized. Addicted to the thrill. As gone as all the visions of the freakouts and the acidheads. Turned on to death and tragedy. The world in self-destruct.

Purgation's now a laxative. No longer do we flush the spirit. The private entity of flesh and feel. Of sex. Of food. Elimination and consumption. Of murder and creation. Death and Birth and Nudity. Publicity of all that's private. Or once was. As nothing sacred is. Which profanity would not profane. As theatre for a culture that's turned on tuned in engrossed in all the wrap-around of musical chairs. The game's called exploit or be exploited. Lie or be shafted. And soon the dreams of youth and man and woman. Of sex and truth. And even maybe art. The Logos and the Color and the Sound. Will be all banked for us. And sealed. For us to push the button. As we do for News and Murder now. And Death and Sex and Life and Art. Will be all one. The flavor and the savor. Of a trip to dreamland. As we freak out. *Alle and somme.* And wonder. If we do. Or care at all. As we blast off. Tune in. What it might have been. To know or be. In the story of the *once-upon-a-time.* So now full of fiction-of-the-all-around-us-world. What the Real Thing. Really was. The TRUTH. Not like it was. Or as it was. But WAS.

ABOUT THE AUTHOR

ARLENE ZEKOWSKI WAS FIRST introduced to the arts at an early age at her grandfather's art and auction galleries on Long Island and in Brooklyn. Awarded a graduate scholarship at Brooklyn College for her writing and editorship of the French arts journal L'Etincelle, she later received an M.A. in 1945 on a fellowship at Duke University, with a study of André Gide. She taught modern languages and literature at Queens College, University of Connecticut, Champlain and Mohawk Colleges, worked in New York as an editorial assistant, and in New Jersey as a statehouse correspondent for the Atlantic City Daily World. *During World War II she was with the United States government Lend-Lease program.*

While traveling in England and on the Continent, and living in Paris from 1948 to 1951, her first book Thursday's Season *was published.*

In 1952 she met and married the author Stanley Berne in New York. Their collaborative work A First Book of the Neo-Narrative, *published in 1954, with a preface by Donald Sutherland and critical commentary by William Carlos Williams, earned them the friendship and support of Marianne Moore, Henry Miller, Thornton Wilder, Anais Nin, Janet Flanner, Waldo Frank, and Sir Herbert Read who prefaced her 1964 book* Abraxas..

In 1957, New World Writing #11's Zekowski and Berne feature "The End of Story in the Novel" also previewed their 1958 Cardinals & Saints *volume, attracting artist Milton Avery who subsequently illustrated Zekowski's 1962 book,* Concretions.

After a graduate fellowship at Louisiana State University, the author was appointed to a teaching post at Eastern New Mexico University in 1963, where she was the recipient of numerous literature grants. She is presently Research Associate Professor in the Center for Advanced Professional Studies and Research.

In 1981 she co-hosted and co-produced (with Stanley Berne) the 9 part television series Future Writing Today, *now being shown over many PBS stations.*

Arlene Zekowski is related to the 19th century Russian poet, Vasíly Zhukóvsky.

(Cf. Contemporary Authors, New Revision Series, *Vol. 1, p. 733)*